SPACE, TIME, AND INFINITY

Essays on
Fantastic Literature

by

Brian Stableford

The Borgo Press
An Imprint of Wildside Press

MMVII

I.O. Evans Studies in the Philosophy and Criticism of Literature
ISSN 0271-9061

Number Thirty-Eight

Library of Congress Cataloging in Publication Data:

Stableford, Brian M.
    Space, time, and infinity: essays on fantastic literature / by Brian Sta-
bleford.
    p. cm. — (I.O. Evans studies in the philosophy & criticism of litera-
ture, ISSN 0271-9061 ; no. 38)
    Includes bibliographical references and index.
    ISBN 0-8095-0911-3 (cloth). – ISBN 0-8095-1911-9 (pbk.)
    1. Fantastic literature, English—History and criticism. 2. Fantastic lit-
erature, American—History and criticism. 3. Science fiction, American—History and criticism. 4. Science fiction, English—History and
criticism. 5. Space and time in literature. 6. Infinite in literature. I. Title.
II. Series.
PR408.F34S69 2007   98-45501
809'.915—dc 21   CIP

FIRST EDITION

CONTENTS

INTRODUCTION

With one exception, the talks and essays collected in this volume were all written after I acquired a word-processor. I mention this because the possession of such an instrument inevitably changes the way a writer operates, and because at least some of those changes have left an easily-distinguishable mark on several of the items included here.

Nowadays, when I have to deliver a lecture or am commissioned to write an essay on a particular topic, my first recourse is to lift relevant chunks of material out of other talks or essays which I happen to have on disk. It often happens that I deliver a similarly-titled talk four or five times to different audiences (SF conventions, university SF societies, clients of a public library, etc.), reworking its substance every time. Even when I become bored with a topic and decide to move on I am likely to carry forward elements which seem to be worth elaboration or reconsideration. For this reason, my non-fiction work has come to resemble an elaborate patchwork in which certain motifs recur, subtly altering their form as they move from one location to another.

I have attempted to select the contents of this volume in such a way as to minimize these overlaps and reiterations but the reader will undoubtedly experience the occasional sensation of *déjà-vu*. I hope that this will not prove too irritating, and that it might even be piquantly interesting to some readers.

"Setting Ideas in Space, Time, and Infinity" was written for a two-day science fiction event held at an Arts Centre in Cardiff in 1989, arranged by local resident, the Reverend Lionel Fanthorpe. Lionel has been my friend for many years, although I did not meet him for some time after the conclusion of his now-legendary career writing science fiction novels and supernatural stories for Badger Books. Although he is now a minister of the Church of Wales while I remain a deeply-committed atheist, we continue to enjoy one another's company and to exchange ironies like those contained in the introduction to the talk. This is the first time it has appeared in print, partly because of it borrowings from other published items. "The Necessity of Science Fiction," which was a guest-of-honor speech delivered at ConFuse 1 in Linkoping, Sweden in 1992, belongs to the same chain of recut-and-repasted talks and is similarly unpublished in this particular form.

"The British and American Traditions of Speculative Fiction" was the after-lunch speech delivered when I was the "guest scholar" at the International Conference on the Fantastic in the Arts in Houston in 1987; it was reprinted in a volume of papers selected from the conference called *Contours of the Fantastic* edited by Michele K. Langford, published by Greenwood Press in 1990. It is mainly a summary of the argument of my history of *Scientific Romance in Britain, 1890-1950*—whose publication presumably inspired the invitation from the ICFA—but the final part does add some new observations on continuing contrasts between the typical concerns and mannerisms of British and American science fiction.

The one item in the collection which was first written before I acquired a word-processor is "The Biology and Sociology of Alien Worlds," which is the text of an open lecture given at the University of York in 1985; it was, however, put on disk and slightly revised in order that it might be reprinted in the journal *Social Biology and Human Affairs*, where it appeared in vol. 52, no. 1 (1988).

"Cosmic Perspectives in Nineteenth-Century Literature" was a paper presented at a symposium on the work and influence of Edgar Allan Poe, held at the "Centre for the Study of Metaphor" in the University of Nice in 1987; it was reprinted in the proceedings of the conference, *Actes du troisième colloque international de science-fiction de Nice* in the journal *Métaphores* #15-16 (Janvier 1988).

"An Introduction to Alternate Worlds" was written for the first issue of a fanzine edited by Michael Morton, whose creation was prompted by the formation of an Internet discussion group. Although it is an elaboration of the entry on "Alternate Worlds" which I did for the second edition of John Clute's *Encyclopedia of Science Fiction* (Orbit, 1993) it benefits from somewhat wider research, which was greatly assisted by a magnificently comprehensive bibliography of alternate history stories that had been compiled by members of the Internet discussion group, including Robert Schmunk and Evelyn C. Leeper. The article first appeared in *Alternate Worlds* #1 (January 1994)

"Adolf Hitler: His Part in Our Struggle: (A Brief Economic History of British SF Magazines)" was commissioned by David Pringle for the tenth anniversary issue of *Interzone* and appeared in *Interzone* #57 (March 1992). *"The Battle of Dorking* and Its Aftermath" was written for the same periodical, extending a series of essays on "Yesterday's Bestsellers" which had begun in *Million: The Magazine About Popular Fiction*, but was briefly continued in *Interzone* after the demise of *Million* in order to provide an element of continuity for those subscribers whose subscriptions had to be transferred to the sister magazine. It first appeared in *Interzone* #83 (May 1994).

"The Science in Science Fiction" was a talk written for the annual "Christmas event" held at the Science Museum, which took SF as its theme in 1993. It was reprinted in the *Beneluxcon 20 Souvenir Book* in April 1994. "The Siren Song of Sexuality" was the introduction to an anthology called *The Dedalus Book of Femmes Fatales* which I edited for the small press in question; it was originally published in 1992.

"What We Know About Vampires" was written for a special vampire issue of Angela Readman's Gothic fanzine *The Penny Dreadfull*; it appeared in issue no. 4 in September 1995.

"A Brief History of Vampires" and "A Brief History of Werewolves" were commissioned by the editors of a horror magazine called *The Dark Asylum*. Rumor has it that the first item was actually published in the second issue of the magazine but I never saw a copy; the editors never sent out complimentary copies or paid the contributors and seem to

7

have vanished from human ken. The second article, which is published here for the first time, reproduces some material from an earlier article called "Animal Spirits: The Erotic and the Supernatural in Michael Jackson's Thriller video," which was reprinted in my Borgo Press collection *Algebraic Fantasies and Realistic Romances* (1995), but I thought it sufficiently different to warrant separate reprinting.

—Brian Stableford
Reading, England

I.

SETTING IDEAS IN
SPACE, TIME, AND INFINITY

When my good friend Lionel Fanthorpe used to write SF novels for Badger Books the titles were given to him along with the commissioning notes. He clearly still feels that this is the way things ought to be done, because he generously supplied this title to me without wasting any time in prior consultation. I have, of course, been happy to accept it, though I must confess that I have unresolved doubts about the precise implications of the phrase "space, time and infinity," and I hope that you will not feel too disappointed if, at the end of this discourse, you are still wondering where and when infinity can possibly be, if it is not in space or time.

I am grateful for the originality which Lionel has shown in using his initiative to invert a particularly tedious question which SF writers are asked far too frequently: where do we get our ideas from? There is a certain charming novelty in being asked to explain not where SF writers find their ideas, but how they decide where to put them.

This is a clever variation, because it forbids me to draw upon the repertoire of stock answers which SF writers have developed in order to deal with the former question briefly and sarcastically. For instance, when Harlan Ellison is asked where he gets his ideas from he tends to tell people that he gets them on subscription from an ideas service in Schenectady, which sends him a batch of newly-hatched ideas on the first of every month. I generally just come clean and admit that I steal my ideas, though I usually add a modest aside to the effect that when I become really desperate because I can't find an appropriate idea to steal, I have to resort to the sneakier strategy of making them up.

No such slick and ready-made answer springs immediately to mind as a suitable response to the question of how I decide what sort of setting will show off my ideas to best advantage, and to admit that most of them end up in the waste-paper bin would undoubtedly be a frivolous avoidance of the issue.

The business of trying to find a sensible answer to the question is complicated by the fact that there is no very clear distinction, in science fiction and fantasy, between ideas and settings. When dealing with other genres it is relatively easy to talk about "settings" as a separate issue—a murder mystery or a love story might plausibly be set in any one of a whole series of actual locations or actual historical periods without overmuch modification to the basic pattern of the plot, whereas a western can hardly be set anywhere else but on the American frontier—but SF and fantasy are more confusing.

If by the "ideas" in science fiction and fantasy stories we mean the things in them which the author invents, we will find that in some cases—but not all—the settings are ideas. Sometimes, it is true, a science fiction author will come up with an idea which he could in principle locate within any of a number of different settings—so that, for instance, when Theodore Sturgeon wanted to write about a society of hermaphrodite humans he chose to set his story in the future, whereas when Ursula K. Le Guin wanted to write about a similar situation she chose to establish it on another world. But it might equally well be the case that a writer's starting point will be a desire to imagine how colonists might set up home on Mars, or what kind of living things might have evolved in the atmosphere of Jupiter. In all of these cases, the task of integrating ideas, plots and settings into some sort of coherent whole requires careful thought and a good deal of supplementary invention.

The setting of a science fiction or fantasy story is very often the chief item of invention in it. Even when a story revolves around some other central notion, like an imaginary machine or a hypothetical society, the setting has still to be imagined and constructed in such a fashion that it can sensibly contain the idea. Writers of mundane fiction may well have to do a good deal of creative work to build a convincing setting for their stories, but their problems can usually be solved by discovery and research; writers of fantastic stories are routinely faced by problems of an entirely different order.

Mundane fiction, which deals with the world as it is and was, has both advantages and disadvantages by virtue of being bound to settings which are already contained within the accepted wisdom of geography and history. The main advantage for the writer is that he can base his descriptions on ones which already exist, and need not do very much in the way of description if he doesn't want to, because his readers are already thoroughly familiar with the world in which his story is set. The main disadvantage is that he is tightly bound by those descriptions and that familiarity. A writer of such fictions does have a certain artistic licence to tamper with the world, which may allow the invention of imaginary institutions, towns, or even minor nation-states, but propriety demands that such inventions be kept under strict control.

Writers who elect to use imaginary settings cannot benefit as much from background research or from assumptions about the reader's familiarity. There may well be scientific knowledge which will help them to put together an imaginary world in a sensible fashion, and it is also the case that readers do have some knowledge of certain standard scenarios in SF and fantasy, and are therefore capable of identifying and quickly cultivating an understanding of many such scenarios when they are rudely pitched into one. Even so, writers of such stories must be prepared to give their reader quite a lot of information about the specific settings to be used in the story, and readers of such stories must be prepared to take it all in. On the other hand, the writers and readers of imaginative fiction are unfettered by the oppressiveness of actual history, geography and social life—only they can boldly go where no one has ever actually gone; only they can be pioneering explorers of infinite possibility.

11

* * * * * * *

There are, of course, some SF and fantasy stories which do require a strong measure of fidelity to known fact. Some science fiction stories are set in the immediate or very near future, in a world whose history, geography and social life are the same as our own—until that critical moment arrives when the alien invaders land or World War III breaks out or the vital experiment goes tragically wrong.

There is a grey area in which science fiction of this kind overlaps with spy stories and straightforward thrillers. Its borderline is that kind of science fiction in which a major disruption of the world is threatened, but ultimately prevented by the destruction of the threat, so that the plot of the story ends up where it began, in the world as known and understood. That kind of science fiction is often suspenseful, but it is guilty of a kind of imaginative cowardice. Bolder writers are not concerned with saving the world from change; they are concerned instead to investigate the possible transformations of the world which would stem from the things which they invent.

Many writers of this more adventurous kind do not even want to start their stories in the world-as-known; they want to hurl themselves and their readers straight into futures remote from our own, into worlds which have already been dramatically altered by historical and technological change. Others do not want to concern themselves with our world at all, but with other worlds, which have wholly invented histories and geographies, and whose inhabitants may be very different from us in terms of their society and their biology. In stories like these, the business of constructing an interesting and plausible setting is very different from the kind of period reproduction which is used to establish the settings of mundane fiction.

There is another kind of science fiction story which remakes the past, by substituting for the history of our world an alternative history which diverged from ours because of some crucial alteration of a past event. There are, for instance, many stories which try to imagine how the world might have turned out had Hitler been victorious in World War II.

Here too, fidelity to actual history is an important consideration, not simply because the world of the story shares with ours the history preceding the altered event, but also because there is much which the altered event would leave unchanged, or would modify in a relatively slight fashion. Again, some works which confine themselves to very trivial alterations of history lie on the very borders of the SF genre, little different from the general run of thrillers. As before, though, the most adventurous exercises of this kind want to change the world very dramatically, and are ambitious to deal with alternative pasts and presents which are strikingly different from our own.

There are also some kinds of fantasy fiction which are closely related to mundane fiction in terms of their settings. Horror stories usually deal with the disruption of the ordinary lived-in world by some malevolent supernatural agency, and they are horrific precisely because of that breakdown of normality. Like near-future science fiction—with which modern horror fiction overlaps considerably—horror stories must start with a careful representation of the world as it is, and it is much more common in horror fiction than in science fiction for the end of the story to be a restoration of that normal and comfortable world.

It is, in fact, relatively rare for horror stories to deal with permanent large-scale transfigurations of the world, and this ties horror stories much more closely than other kinds of imaginative fiction to the criteria of propriety which apply to mundane fiction. By contrast, the kinds of fiction which are nowadays marketed under the label "fantasy"—which include what used to be called "heroic fantasy" or "sword and sorcery" fiction—tend to be set in what J. R. R. Tolkien calls Secondary Worlds.

Secondary Worlds are often not very clearly located in space and time. Sometimes they are worlds which exist, in some frankly mysterious sense, in parallel with our own, so that the characters can travel between our world and the other via doorways which can be located in a mirror or a wardrobe or anywhere else that the author happens to find convenient. Sometimes Secondary Worlds are accessible only in dreams, so that they belong to the world of the mind rather than the universe at large. More often, though, they are presumed to exist, as it were, in place of our own world, with a sun which rises and sets as ours does, having much the same atmosphere and climate as ours, and often having a fairly similar history to ours. What makes these worlds of fantasy crucially different from ours is not that they dis-placed from it in time or space—as the imaginary worlds of science fiction are—but that they are worlds where some kind of magic works.

In much the same way that there is an overlap be-tween near-future science fiction, horror stories and contem-porary thrillers, there is also an overlap between fantasy fic-tion and mundane historical fiction. This comes about for two reasons. Firstly, what we know of the remoter history of our own world is inextricably confused with myth and leg-end, so that authors who set stories in the distant past have much wider creative options in formulating settings than au-thors who deal with times and places about which much more is known. Secondly—and, in this context, more impor-tantly—the people who lived even in recent times past did believe in various supernatural entities and acted in accor-dance with those beliefs; it is therefore easily possible to write stories which are faithful to known historical fact in all respects save for the supposition that the characters' beliefs about magic, witches and demons had some substance.

In recent years there has been a certain amount of sniping between science fiction writers and fantasy writers as to whose is the most worthy activity. Science fiction writers sometimes argue that writing fantasy is easier, because "any-thing goes," while science fiction must be logical. Their case has been succinctly summed up by Gregory Benford, who once remarked that writing fantasy instead of science fiction is like playing tennis without the net. Fantasy writers, an-noyed by the implied contempt for their art, argue in their turn that what they do can be every bit as rigorous as SF. They point out that just as there is a species of "hard science fiction" which deals rigorously with the extrapolation of real technology and requires considerable expertise, so there is a species of "hard fantasy" which deals rigorously with the magical world-views of actual past societies and requires just as much scholarly expertise. This "hard fantasy" operates very close to the borderline between fantasy and historical fiction, though its more ambitious writers are willing to make gross transformations of known history in painstakingly extrapolating the hypothesis that magic works.

It is perhaps also worth mentioning in connection with this overlap between fantasy and historical fiction that there is a subgenre of historical fiction which might be called "demythologized fantasy," in which apparently-fantastic stories borrowed from myth and legend are retold in such a way that all the supernatural elements of the original stories are "explained away."

* * * * * *

Having considered these various ways in which the settings of science fiction and fantasy diverge in several directions from the settings of mundane fiction, we must also note that in the realms of pure imagination there is also a significant overlap between the Secondary Worlds of fantasy and the alien worlds of science fiction (which are sometimes represented as parallel worlds displaced in "other dimensions"). This is inevitable for several reasons, which have spilled over from certain strategies which writers have used to enhance the plausibility of their fiction into the marketing strategies employed by publishers, who have tried to import into common usage the term "science fantasy." Because this overlap is of particular significance to the remainder of my argument, I should like to consider the reasons for it fairly carefully.

One important reason for this confusion of SF and fantasy scenarios is that writers of action-adventure science fiction inevitably find it convenient to deal with worlds which are not too alien—worlds where human beings can breathe and move about easily, and can undergo adventures without too much difficulty. The popularity of early SF adventures in which human beings had colorful adventures on Venus or Saturn, without the authors taking any real consideration of the likely differences of atmosphere and certain differences of gravity, is not really to be explained by the supposition that people really thought that Venus and Saturn were just cloudier versions of the earth. The point is that writers needed somewhere to set that kind of colorful adventure, and Venus and Saturn were as convenient as anywhere else until the time when collective consciousness of their unsuitability was so far raised that such a cavalier attitude became unacceptable—at which time it became politic for other settings (like "parallel worlds" or the worlds of other stars) to be substituted.

Another important factor in the overlap is that the jargon of magical fantasy and the jargon of science fiction are in some important respects virtually interchangeable. Science fiction writers have very often been prepared to admit into their stories most of the things which magicians were traditionally supposed to be able to do, so long as the abilities in question are suitably camouflaged by the kind of pseudoscientific jargon which speaks of "extra-sensory perceptions," "telepathy" and "psychokinesis." This kind of jargonized magic is one of the staples of "science fantasy," and helps to make much notional SF set in the far-flung outposts of the galaxy very similar in the manner of its action and the tone of its writing to fantasy set in Secondary Worlds.

* * * * * * *

To recapitulate briefly, we have seen that in both science fiction and fantasy, there are works which begin, and sometimes end, in the world-as-known, and there are other works which are careful never to stray far from the world-as-known. In these works, as in stories of the near future or contemporary horror stories, the plausibility of at least some of the settings used must be assured by the same methods which assure the plausibility of settings in mundane fiction. By the same token, though, there can be found in both genres stories whose main ambition is to deal with settings which are invented rather than researched, imaginary rather than historical. The most adventurous works in both genres may require the creation and description of whole new worlds—

but we must add to this the cautionary rider that a great many of the supposedly imaginary worlds of science fiction are in fact very similar to one another, and are in fact simply earth-clones whose inhabitants can do magic.

How, then, do authors go about the business of creating the more exotic settings of SF and fantasy: the further futures, the more alien worlds, the less-stereotyped Secondary Worlds?

Statistically speaking, the answer is simple enough—the great majority of writers steal them, contenting themselves with making mainly cosmetic modifications to templates which already exist. Ninety-five per cent of the books which you will see on the racks at any one time have settings which are ninety-five per cent second hand. This is, however, by no means the wholesale crime which use of the word "steal" might imply, and perhaps it is misleading to use it—though "borrow," "imitate" and other euphemisms are just as misleading.

The reason that such words are misleading is that almost all the settings used in science fiction and fantasy are to some degree conventional, and it could not be otherwise. To a large extent, the imaginary settings of SF and fantasy are shared property in much the same way that mundane settings are available to anybody who cares to use them. Most of the features of imaginary settings tend to be the product of long historical processes of accretion; there is a sense in which science fiction and fantasy writers are always collaborating with their predecessors in bringing forward a collective vision of the universe and its Secondary alternatives.

It is perhaps easiest to see why this must be so in the case of fantasy, whose Secondary Worlds have been shaped over time by the gradual refinement and modification of the once-believed-in Secondary Worlds of myth and legend. The British prototype of the literary Secondary World is the land of Faerie which, according to our folklore, existed alongside ours, from which enigmatic fairy brides occasionally came and into which unlucky mortals occasionally strayed. All the cultures of the ancient world had their own Secondary Worlds, but these were very often significantly similar in important respects—presumably because the functions which they served within each culture were much the same.

Much modern fantasy still deals more-or-less straightforwardly with Secondary Worlds borrowed from particular mythologies, but modern writers are not at all reluctant to invent their own substitutes along similar lines, complete with their own histories, geographies, pantheons of gods and legions of troublesome demons.

There is a sense in which the imaginary worlds of science fiction are similarly inherited, although there has in these cases been a much more obvious process of refinement and modification carried out in the light of the unfolding pattern of scientific discovery. To take the most obvious example, there is a long tradition of speculative fantasies dealing with voyages to the moon, whose modern extension has gradually come to reflect the improvement of our inferences about conditions upon the surface of the moon.

Early lunar romances tended to be entirely satirical, happily embracing the utter absurdity of imagining that the moon might be a world like ours, or that we might one day be able to go there. Such assumptions began to change, though, in the early seventeenth century. John Kepler's *Somnium*, written at that time, attempts quite seriously to describe what the movements of the sun and the planets would look like to an observer on the moon if—as Kepler but not everyone then believed—the sun and not the earth was the central point about which the planets revolved. Kepler then went on to try to imagine what sort of plant and animal life might exist on the moon, given that the length of the day was so very different there—and given also his mistaken assumption that the moon, like the earth, must have an atmosphere.

Since Kepler's day we have seen a whole series of literary responses to new discoveries about the solar system, which have by degrees updated conventional literary images of the planets. One set of discoveries in particular has transformed science fictional imagery: the discovery that the other planets in the solar system are all incapable of sustaining human life—or, indeed, any life with a similar biochemistry. This has forced hard SF writers to come up with in-

18

creasingly sophisticated images of technologically-supported colonies on very hostile worlds, while simultaneously spurring the sciencefictional imagination outwards in search of more hospitable realms—into the further reaches of a universe which was simultaneously expanding, and becoming ever stranger, in the scientific imagination.

If one takes the claims of science fiction writers at face value, the constraints governing this expansion of perspective are logical ones. Their work is supposedly governed by fidelity to the known principles of physics, chemistry and genetics, with which their inventions are not supposed to conflict. In fact, these claims are very largely a sham, and science fiction writers have always been prepared to deploy convenient jargon terms which casually cancel out the most inconvenient of these limitations. The most obvious examples of such jargon are those which are used to excuse the faster-than-light travel which is conventionally employed to give literary access to an infinite supply of alien worlds and an infinite variety of quasi-human societies. Science fiction of this kind is a species of fantasy, whose attempts to claim plausibility on the grounds of staying within the limits of future possibility are a confidence trick. But it is not my intention to insult fantasy, whether it is disguised as science fiction or not—what interests me far more is the question of why fantasies are able to command our interest and how they contrive to convince us that they are plausible.

* * * * * * *

If we are to talk seriously about the plausibility of the more exotic settings which are found in SF and fantasy stories it will be helpful to begin by drawing a distinction between "logical plausibility" and "psychological plausibility."

Logical plausibility demands that a story should extrapolate carefully within some framework of limitations which is taken as axiomatic. Although we associate this kind of plausibility primarily with hard SF stories, fantasy stories should also be reckoned to fail if they are not internally consistent. Once the writer has laid down the basic premises of a fantasy story—however absurd they may be—plausibility is

19

at least partly dependent on his sticking to them, and extrapolating them in a clever fashion.

If we look at things in this way, hard science fiction becomes that species of fantasy which will accept as axioms only notions borrowed from actual scientific thought, or which do not conflict with the image of the universe supplied by scientific thought. (Ironically, it is the stories which try hardest to be faithful to known fact which are most easily betrayed by the march of progress. Arthur C. Clarke's most impressive early attempts at realism—in books like *A Fall of Moondust* and *The Sands of Mars*—have been far more easily invalidated by the revelations of subsequent space exploration than his romantic futuristic fantasies, *The City and the Stars* and *Childhood's End*.)

But the eagerness of hard SF writers to conserve logical plausibility in harness with scientific knowledge, and their loudness in proclaiming the virtues of that magical combination, should not be allowed to blind us to the fact that neither logic nor science has very much to do with the psychological plausibility which largely determines what readers are prepared to believe.

Readers are, of course, widely different in terms of their inherent gullibility, and a failure of logical plausibility which will spoil a story for one reader may easily go unnoticed by many others—but the tolerance which readers display to logical implausibilities is by no means simply a function of their ignorance, as the popularity of self-declared fantasy readily demonstrates. There are other factors involved which allow readers to accept, for literary purposes, things which they could not really bring themselves to believe. This is conventionally recognized by saying that reading fantasy involves "a willing suspension of disbelief." But a proper explanation must go further than this; it must also be noted that there are also certain things which, though logically incoherent or demonstrably impossible, are nevertheless remarkably seductive of real belief.

It is worth noting here that the psychology of probability conflicts in some important respects with the actual mathematics of probability. The fact that a roulette wheel has come up red six times in a row has, in reality, no influence whatsoever on the likelihood that it will come up red again, but the majority of people have some kind of gut feeling which leads them often to assert—and, indeed, sometimes firmly to believe—that after a run of reds, the likelihood of black turning up next time is increased. There are many gambling games which are designed to take account of this and other differences between the psychological perception of probability and the mathematical actualities of probability in seducing punters to take what they believe to be sensible risks but which are actually nothing of the kind.

In much the same way, our psychological perceptions of what the world is like differ in certain important respects from what science has to tell us about what it is actually like. The truth is often less plausible than certain seductive lies and illusions, even when it can be proven.

There are many ideas which crop up regularly in science fiction, and which have been accepted into the conventions of the genre, although they have no logical plausibility whatsoever. One such notion—the time-paradox story in which the changing of a past event cancels out the present from which the changer set out—actually relies for its aesthetic appeal on its own logical impossibility. We enjoy such stories precisely because we discover a conflict between what is psychologically plausible and what is logically nonsensical.

There are certain notions which have been around since time immemorial as items of real belief, whose psychological plausibility is so powerful that it leads people constantly to manufacture evidence of their reality. The notions that people might be able to foresee the future, or to read thoughts in other people's minds, or to move objects by the power of the mind, all belong to this class. The fact that these ideas are in frank conflict with our notions of what is logically possible does not prevent lots of people believing in them wholeheartedly, and it is hardly surprising to find them accepted in science fiction as items which can be plausibly and dramatically extrapolated in images of future society and alien intelligence.

It is, of course, mainly the psychological plausibility of these kinds of ideas which makes fantasy stories so readily believable; fantasies actually require a far less radical willingness to suspend disbelief than science fiction stories which deal with hypotheses which are logically possible but psychologically difficult to accommodate. Psychological plausibility is, at least in some respects, more powerful than logical plausibility.

This should not surprise us. The power of psychological probability to deny and defy logical probability can be fairly easily demonstrated by observing the betting strategies of people who are well aware, at a conscious level, of the independence of events. The vast majority of people who know perfectly well that a run of reds does not make black any more likely to come up next time will still put their money on black—the people who are most likely to bet on red again are not the hardened rationalists but people who believe in quasi-magical runs of luck.

* * * * * * *

These observations have striking repercussions upon the business of inventing settings for all kinds of imaginative fiction. Indeed, they have a considerable bearing on the settings of mundane fiction, whose plausibility is controlled far more by psychological factors than by strict accuracy of representation.

The force exerted upon the imagination by a story can often survive recognition of blatant logical errors. One famous instance of such an error can be found in William Golding's novel *Lord of the Flies*, where the castaway children light fires with the aid of Piggy's spectacles, despite the fact that it is perfectly clear (and necessary to the workings of the plot) that Piggy is short-sighted, and therefore must have spectacles with concave lenses, which are incapable of focusing sunlight to start a fire. Most readers do not notice this, but if and when it is pointed out to them, it does not usually serve to obliterate their feeling that the story as a whole is both powerful and convincing. How unsurprising it is, therefore, to find that the same is generally true of science fiction and fantasy stories—that the discovery therein of logical fudging, or even of blatant logical failure, will not necessarily destroy the sense of plausibility which the reader has, provided that the story is sufficiently in tune with psychological plausibility.

One important conclusion to be drawn from all this is that the setting of a story—whether it be a future earth, an alien world or a Secondary World—depends far more for its plausibility on the kinds of ideas which are deployed there than on the conscientious logical extrapolation of whatever is known or assumed about such settings. The further SF writers attempt to reach into the future or the distant parts of the universe the less they can depend upon the logic of extrapolation to make their stories interesting and readable, and the more they will be tempted to depend, as fantasy writers must, on the psychology of plausibility.

Taken to its extreme—an extreme which is very frequently attained by actual stories—this realisation informs us that the apparent adventurousness of much science fiction and fantasy must often be a sham. If we were to take a pessimistic view of the argument's implications, we would begin to wonder whether the greater ambitions of imaginative fiction might in fact be hopeless, on the grounds that what we can most easily bring ourselves to believe when we stretch our imaginations towards their limits is what we are most heavily psychologically predisposed to believe: which is to say, the most fundamental and infantile of our notions.

That this fear is not groundless is demonstrated by the depressing profusion of *Star Trek* episodes in which we boldly go to the edge of the universe only to find the same boring ideas that are predominant in the oldest recorded fairy tales. This unfortunate plunge from grandiosity to absurdity is perhaps seen to most spectacular disadvantage in the cinematic extravaganza *2001*, written by Arthur C. Clarke and directed by Stanley Kubrick, whose final image— following a supposed journey to the far edge of possibility— is a thumb-sucking embryo.

I believe, however, that we may legitimately hope to reach a less depressing conclusion than this. I think that science fiction and fantasy do have the capacity to be something other than a ludicrously pretentious contemplation of our cultural umbilical cord.

My hope is based in the conviction that we are in fact capable of using our intelligence to extricate ourselves from the soggy morass of psychological plausibility, and that the first step we must take in so doing is to expose those ideas with which we are most cosily comfortable to confrontation. Such confrontation will hopefully lead on to interrogation and—if we are strong enough to accomplish it—to rational demolition. Science fiction and fantasy offer us a useful method of taking that first step, and their most genuinely ambitious works may also assist us to take the others.

Both science fiction and fantasy provide a means of isolating our most cherished notions by transplanting them into imaginary settings where they cannot help but stand naked and exposed, unclothed by the mass of mundane detail which shelters them in mundane fiction. In doing so, science fiction and fantasy can help to prepare a path by which we may approach serious questions about why we find these ideas so comfortable and so comforting, and what penalties we may incur by treasuring such illusions.

However difficult it is to do it, we must expose psychological plausibility to the rigors of logical analysis, so that we may first of all explain it as a phenomenon, and then do our best to transcend it. That is the path of intellectual progress.

Only a minority of stories will ever try to help us in this quest, let alone achieve some measure of success. Unfortunately, those stories will by necessity seem to the majority of their readers to be threatening, subversive and discomfiting. Most writers will always settle, in designing and playing with their settings, for the easy option of pandering to psychological plausibility, cosily flattering the misapprehensions of that majority of readers. In my view, though, it is the discomfiting minority of stories that aspire to expose and trouble the limits of our psychological cowardice which justifies the ambitions of science fiction and fantasy, and makes those genres worthwhile.

II.

THE NECESSITY OF
SCIENCE FICTION

It was recently my pleasure and my privilege to attend the annual meeting of the World SF organization, which was held in Chengdu, China. In connection with the meeting the hosts organized a conference at which papers were alternately presented by Chinese and foreign delegates. This conference was seen as a very important event by its organizers and domestic participants, many of whom evidently hoped that its occurrence would help to set Chinese SF on the road to an intellectual respectability which it had hitherto been denied.

The causes of that denial, as the Chinese delegates took great pains to explain, are complex. Partly, they are linguistic: the Chinese phrase into which the Western term "science fiction" is translated is closer in spirit to "science fantasy," which seems to many Chinese intellectuals to be unhealthily oxymoronic. Partly, they are sociological: as a nation still in the process emerging from Third World status, China has numerous professional scientists and technologists capable of writing SF, but has no larger public sufficiently educated in science to provide an interested and critical audience. Partly, they are historical: extreme Marxism is hostile to anything which is imaginatively adventurous, and during the years of the so-called Cultural Revolution, from 1968 until 1978, emergent Chinese SF was banned and some of its writers were sent to collective farms in order that they might be re-educated into a proper understanding of the error of their ways. Thankfully, the most influential of them was able to resist this re-education, and was able to attend the conference to demonstrate that although his health had been ruined his mind remained as sharp as ever.

This multiplicity of causes serves to make the problem difficult of solution, and one can only hope that the fact of the conference having taken place does indeed help. Unfortunately, the content of the papers given by the foreign guests—all of whom had arrived without any forewarning of what might be expected of them—did nothing substantial to contribute to this cause. Mine, hastily prepared, and even more hastily revised when I realized the conditions under which it would have to be delivered, with pauses at the end of each sentence to allow a translator to render it into Chinese as best he could, was no exception. Even though any comment which I might have made would have been of paltry significance, I felt that this was a pity, especially in view of the fact that I had on various previous occasions delivered speeches whose function was to insist, in the face of the contempt in which it is usually held even in the West, that science fiction is not merely intellectually respectable but vitally necessary, as a mental instrument which can and will enable us to deal more effectively with a future which seems more threatening with every year that passes.

One day, perhaps, I might be able to return to China, better able to lend my small voice to the Herculean task which faces the advocates of science fiction in that country. In the meantime, I am even more convinced than I was before that whenever and wherever science fiction writers are given a platform, they should use that opportunity for arguing, with all the force and vehemence they can muster, that science fiction is something important, which does not deserve the contempt in which it is so frequently held. I am aware in saying this, of course, that there is much that is published under the science fiction label which is utterly trivial, and much that is devoid of any vestige of intellectual respectability, and that SF—like any popular genre—is always apt to be judged and condemned by outsiders on the weakness of its worst examples rather than the strength of its best. However, I do believe that the best contemporary science fiction is, both intellectually and aesthetically, of a very high standard, and that it fully deserves to be acknowledged as one of the most interesting and admirable cultural products of our time. In this speech—and, I hope, many subsequent speeches—I will try to explain why.

If we are to address the question of why science fiction is necessary, we must first address the question of why any kind of fiction is necessary. Why is it that we do not and cannot concern ourselves only with matters of fact and probability? Why do we feel compelled—for it is a compulsion, and no mere self-indulgence—to make up stories for ourselves, and tell them to one another?

We all know that stories are exciting, and moving. They have the power to thrill us, to frighten us, to make us happy, or to make us weep. Why is this? Why do we care so much about what happens to characters who do not exist? Why does it make us joyful when an imaginary character in a story achieves his heart's desire, and why can we experience such a sharp sensation of sorrow when, instead, the unfolding logic of events within a story brings its protagonist inexorably to destruction?

We must remember, of course, that we only care about some imaginary characters in such a way that we can rejoice in their successes and weep over their frustrations and failures. There are other characters to whose fate we remain indifferent, and there are some—the villains of the piece—whose successes will cause us pain and whose ultimate destruction will give us tremendous satisfaction.

What is it about those characters with whom we identify which makes them sympathetic, seducing us into caring deeply about their fortunes, and hoping fervently for their ultimate success? It is not that they are like us—at least, not in any simple sense. Anyone who has sat in an audience watching Walt Disney's film *Bambi*, or Steven Spielberg's film *E.T.*, or J. M. Barrie's play *Peter Pan* will have seen large numbers of people reduced to tears by the plight of imaginary characters who bear very little physical resemblance to us—so little, in fact, that the part of *E.T.* is played by a plastic doll and the part of Tinkerbell in *Peter Pan* by a spotlight. The converse is equally true; we do not hate villains because they are alien—indeed, the hunters who shoot

27

Bambi's mother, the men who hunt for E.T., and Captain Hook in *Peter Pan* are all far more closely akin to us than their exotic victims are.

The reason why we have such considerable sympathy for these non-human characters, while we righteously loathe the all-too-human foes who threaten them, clearly has nothing to do with biological similarity. It is purely a matter of moral compatibility. We identify with them because they are nice: friendly, utterly innocent of any intention to do harm, and willing to help others. By the same token, we hate their persecutors because they are not nice: they are violent, uncaring or frankly malevolent. The simple fact is that we love the good guys, whoever and whatever they may be, and we hate the bad guys. The nature and utility of stories is intricately bound up with our ideas of morality.

The universe in which we live does not distribute its rewards and punishments according to any discernible moral order. As St. Matthew and everyone else has observed, the rain falls on the just and the unjust alike. The wicked are no more likely than the good to be struck by lightning or devoured by cancer, and the virtuous are in no way protected by their innocence from suffering and misfortune.

This is a prospect so horrific that one of the principal occupations of the human imagination throughout history has been to support the pretence that the absence from the world of moral order is mere appearance and not reality. The human mind is strongly attracted to the notion that there exists behind and beyond the world of appearances a good God—albeit one who moves in very mysterious ways—and that there will be another life after death where the moral account-books will be belatedly balanced and we will all get what we really deserve. This occupation of the human imagination is really only a special, and arguably rather silly, sub-category of a wider and generally more sensible occupation: the making up of stories.

The world of fiction is intrinsically and necessarily different from the world in which we find ourselves. Virtuous and wicked characters are creations of an author, who is in sole charge of what happens to them, and who can distribute rewards and punishments within his story exactly as he

28

wishes. If, in a story, the virtuous suffer and the wicked flourish, that is no mere accident—it is because the author has determined that things turn out that way. This is not an absence of moral order, but a refusal.

There is no way that an author can avoid moral responsibility for his fictional world and its characters. He may decide to throw dice to decide what happens next, and to whom, but that too is a refusal—a deliberate abandonment of moral prerogative. This is why the reader of a story can and does expect that the ideal movement of a narrative will be towards the success of the sympathetic characters, and knows that when this success is refused, a calculated violation of moral order has been committed, which calls upon him to recognize and lament the horrors of misfortune and wickedness. When such a calculated violation is committed by an author, we call the result "tragedy."

Once we have recognized all of this, we are in a better position to understand some of the commonplace aspects of reading behavior. We can understand, for instance, why most people would rather read stories with happy endings than downbeat stories. Pain is good for us, while it functions as a warning, but no one wants an unrelieved diet of it; we can, by contrast, stand any amount of joy and reassurance. We can also understand why it is that so many readers like to read the same kind of book repeatedly, even though they know exactly what to expect. What these readers are doing is participating in a ritual of moral affirmation whose force depends on repetition, and which is akin to other kinds of affirmative rituals maintained in our society and others: religious, legal and magical rituals are mostly of this kind. We should also be able to understand that when an audience rises to its collective feet and cheers wildly as the villain in a story goes bloodily to his destruction, it is not because its members are latent sadists, but simply because they recognize a ritual moral propriety in what is happening. This fact is unfortunately overlooked in most discussions about the role and effects of violence in the media, which is why most of those discussions are futile.

At a more fundamental level, these observations about the relationship of fiction to morality help us to understand why stories exist at all, and how vital they are to life in human communities. The arts of story-telling were the first tools which people acquired for exploring the question of how we ought to use such limited power as we have to make our lives and our world better; they still remain vitally important tools for use in that way. Stories are all the more important if we are prepared to recognize, as we ought to be, that there is no moral order already laid down for us as if engraved on stone by a careful creator. Moral order is something which must itself be created, decided and continually refined, and stories are part of the instrumentality of that creation and refinement. People who believe otherwise are, of course, hostile to story-tellers.

The problematic relationship between the intrinsic moral order of fiction and the apparent moral neutrality of the universe has an interesting parallel in terms of meaning. Human rationality depends upon our powers of foresight; it is because we can anticipate the probable outcomes of different courses of action that we can make intelligent choices. Our powers of foresight are, however, limited. Events in the world are bound by scientific laws, and can be analysed in terms of cause and effect, but this does not mean that we can predict the outcome of every situation, because the information available to us is almost always incomplete. In the vast majority of situations, we only know some of what we would need to know in order to calculate accurately what the outcome of the situation will be, and must guess the rest as best we can. Life is therefore a kind of gambling game, in which we try to estimate the probabilities as well as we can, but in which much must be left to chance.

It is so uncomfortable to live under the dominion of chance that we are ever avid to improve our predictive skills. This gives us an intense interest in practical science, but it also gives us an intense interest in various kinds of divination. Human beings are forever trying to predict the unpredictable, to discover patterns and trends even where none actually exist. People have always searched their environment for omens, and have been relentless in their quest to discover trustworthy oracles.

Even when we know better than to put our trust in omens and oracles it is difficult to avoid fascination with them; it is not really surprising that astrology, tarot reading and various other kinds of fortune-telling continue to survive and thrive alongside science. Nor is it surprising that we should constantly be trying to interpret our dreams, as determined to find some hidden meaning within their apparent confusion as we are to discover the covert laws which underlie the mysteries of the material world.

In exactly the same way that events in stories cannot be free of moral weight, because the author is the sole governor of what will happen, so events in stories cannot be free of hidden meaning. If a character in a story has a dream, it is entirely up to the author to decide what the events of the dream symbolize, and whether or not the dream will be in some way prophetic. If a character in a story visits a fortune-teller, it is entirely up to the author to decide how much and what kind of meaning can be attached to the cards or the tea-leaves or the entrails which the fortune-teller consults. If the dream or the oracle turns out to mean nothing, that is a refusal, not an absence. The overwhelming probability is, of course, that in a story the dream or the oracle will be meaningful; if it were not, there would be no point in its inclusion. In stories, in fact, all kinds of events can take on symbolic significance, and everything that happens in a story is likely to be meaningful.

In spite of Freud's best efforts, we still have not the slightest idea whether real dreams are meaningful or not, or what they might mean if they are; but literary dreams are a different matter. In stories, dreams are always significant of something; they are always intrinsic parts of the pattern which we call the plot. The world of fiction is full of meanings which are absent from the real world, just as the world of fiction is full of moral rewards and punishments which are absent from the real world.

In certain respects, of course, science fiction is no different from any other kind of fiction in terms of the moral order which it represents and the meanings which it contains. Indeed, much of what is labelled science fiction is simply other kinds of fiction in disguise, and its futuristic or other-worldly trappings are no more than fancy costumes. Nevertheless, true science fiction—which is to say, fiction which which attempts to build logically coherent imaginary worlds based on premises licensed by the world-view of contemporary science—does exhibit some unique and interesting features in its relationship to moral order and questions of meaning.

Stories, as I have pointed out, cannot help but be fundamentally engaged with questions of moral order, but different genres of fiction—by virtue of the specific apparatus of ideas, characters and settings which each deploys—can and do engage different questions of moral order, and engage them in different ways. If we examine the particular kinds of moral question which science fiction typically raises and explores, we will see that it is capable of getting forthrightly to grips with certain problems in moral philosophy which other kinds of fiction can confront only with difficulty, if at all. Indeed, it seems to me that if we look at science fiction from this viewpoint it is quite obvious that science fiction writing is a very important kind of literary enterprise, which does not at all deserve the contempt in which it is held by many literary men.

One of the most fundamental questions of moral philosophy is how a moral community ought to be defined. To which other entities do we owe moral consideration, and why? In their involvement with this question most stories are hamstrung by their attachment to mundane circumstance. Mundane fiction can ask whether animals have rights and it can present case studies relating to the welfare of the unborn, but it cannot do what moral philosophers have increasingly found themselves forced to do, which is to move beyond mundane examples and ask questions about hypothetical cases.

Fantastic fictions—and it is worth noting that most of the fables and parables produced in the ancient world to encapsulate moral wisdom are fantasies featuring non-human characters—are far more flexible. But magical fantasy, which typically addresses moral problems in a fabular or allegorical fashion, is still restricted by comparison with science fiction, whose vocabulary includes a wide spectrum of sentient machines and alien beings which may be, and sometimes are, developed and employed according to a fairly rigorous logic.

The question of whether, or under what conditions, we would owe moral consideration to an alien or an android may seem to the everyday moralist to be lacking in practical relevance, and of course it is—but if we are to work out of proper definition of what is moral and what is not, and to decide what it is that entitles other entities to moral consideration, then we must get to grips with such hypothetical issues. If we are properly to pose the question of what it is which determines whether another entity should or should not belong to our moral community, and if we are properly to explore the feelings which we could and might have towards potential candidates for membership in our moral community, then we cannot do so without reference to sciencefictional constructs like intelligent machines and alien beings. It is no surprise to find that modern exercises in moral philosophy frequently avail themselves of sciencefictional imagery, because the questions which they address demand it. I do not say simply that science fiction stories are useful in this regard, I say that they are necessary.

Another moral question—one of considerable importance in political philosophy—with which science fiction is uniquely fitted to deal, is the question of what we can or ought to mean by the word "progress."

The characters in stories with whom we identify, and to whose causes we attach ourselves, usually have ambitions which transcend the merely personal. Even when their sole purpose within the plot is to unravel a murder mystery or to find true love, their eventual success is symbolic of something larger, affirming some vital principle of justice or some deeply-felt belief about what is worthwhile in human existence. The protagonists of most stories are, therefore, not to be reckoned as mere individuals at all, but as heroes.

A protagonist becomes a true hero when the problem with which he (it may equally well, of course, be she and my use of the masculine should not be taken to apply otherwise) is faced is not merely his own, but that of a larger group. A hero operates on behalf of others; his projects have moral weight for the whole community. In the days of the first stories, a hero operated on behalf of his family or his tribe; more recent heroes usually do the same, although the possibility now exists that they may act on behalf of their nation, or even some vaguely-constituted international community.

The change of state which a hero attempts to bring about is, at least by implication, collective rather than individual, and a successful change of state is one to which we can legitimately attach the label of "progress." One can speak of "progress" in respect of the individual, the tribe or the nation, but nowadays progress usually means the project of mankind taken as a whole—the reconstruction of the entire society of mankind. Although the hero of a story does not often accomplish such a reconstruction, his own endeavors may serve as a model for it, and as an affirmation of its possibility. We do not cheer for the hero because he achieves success for himself, but because his exploits exemplify a kind of success which we desire collectively—because we have glimpsed through the hero the possibility of a better way of life for all.

Just as those philosophers who have tried to determine what it is that entitles an entity to inclusion in a moral community have been inexorably drawn to the deployment of hypothetical entities, so political philosophers who have tried to determine what projects human beings ought to undertake for their collective betterment have been inexorably drawn to the deployment of hypothetical societies—to the imagery of Utopia and Dystopia. At one time such discussions focused entirely on matters of political order and justice, but the idea of moral progress has in the last two hundred years become intricately involved with the idea of technological progress, and it is this involvement which makes science fiction so important as an instrument for the investigation of questions of progress.

The hypothetical societies of the future, and the heroes who embody their dynamic aspects, are impossible to reach through the media of mundane fiction and magical fantasy; only science fiction can confront the myriad hypothetical futures which are conceivable outgrowths of the present. For this reason, the moral questions implicit in the political task of steering the human world into a future replete with threats and opportunities—questions which have become desperately urgent in recent times because of the rapidly-accelerating pace of technological development—are routinely addressed in science fiction. What the heroes of science fiction do, whether their project is to save or to destroy, or merely to survive within the hypothetical societies in which they move, always has implications for the collective decisions real people must make about how to use the technologies which are emerging and evolving around them. There is no more urgent question facing the people of a world which is changing very quickly, and which faces many threats, than the question of how best to foster progress, how best to make use of the opportunities which the advancement of science will open up for us. Again, I do not say simply that science fiction stories are useful in this regard; I say that they are necessary.

As I have already made clear, I cannot believe, or even take seriously the hypothesis, that there is any moral order already built into the universe. In fact, I believe, devoutly and passionately, that the time has come when we must be prepared to give up that dangerous illusion. I think that it is necessary that we should now recognize that the bounds of our moral community and the proper direction of progress are decisions which we have to make, not discoveries which we may make by consulting the appropriate scripture or stone tablet; there may have been a time when that illusion was convenient, but the time has now past. In a fast-changing world—a world where progress is not merely possible but absolutely vital if we are to survive—we cannot afford the kind of moral tyranny which most religions are avid to impose upon us.

Not all religions are equally pernicious in terms of the extent to which they try to short-circuit moral debate, but insofar as religion has served as a generator of dogma and moral absolutism, the hijacking of moral philosophy by religion has been a terrible catastrophe—arguably the worst catastrophe in human history. Attempts to justify notions of good and evil by attaching them to the commandments of imaginary gods have certainly succeeded to some extent in holding moral anarchy at bay, but any apology for religion mounted on those grounds must also take into account the fact that wars of religion and crusades aimed at the extirpation of heresy have created suffering on a scale so frightful that it hardly bears contemplation.

There are, of course, many stories which have been written in order to support one religious dogma or another, and the scriptures of various religions are heavily seasoned with exemplary stories. All fiction, though, by virtue of its very nature, stands in a problematic relationship to religion, because religion's main line of defense against scepticism is an insistence on the absolute and unchallengeable truth of its dogmas. The idea of using fiction as an instrument of moral investigation does not fit in well with fundamentalist views, a fact luridly dramatized by the late Ayatollah Khomeini's response to Salman Rushdie's novel *The Satanic Verses*.

Science fiction stands in a more problematic relationship to religion than other literary genres, not so much because individual science fiction stories present a rigorously secularized view of the universe—that ambition is, alas, very frequently compromised—but because when science fiction is viewed as a genre it cannot help but deny and defy the disease of faith. No matter how many individual science fiction writers may fall prey to that disease, becoming would-be prophets instead of speculators, science fiction taken as a whole will always declare that there is a multitude of possible futures, and that the past of actual history is one of a multitude of alternative histories-that-might-have-been.

By virtue of its multifariousness, science fiction is intrinsically antithetical to the kind of closed thinking which is enshrined in religious fundamentalism. The moral order of science fiction as a genre is logically incompatible with the kind of thinking which declares that there is only one virtuous path for the individual and for mankind, and that adherents of other ways are blasphemers who should be put to death. This is a virtue, and it is a virtue which we desperately need in a world where religious and tribal intolerance generates war, terrorism, hatred and misery on a huge scale. For this reason too, science fiction should be seen not merely as

something intellectually respectable, but as something entirely admirable.

It is convenient here to supplement discussion of
moral order with that of meaning. Here too there is a significant different of emphasis and attitude between science fiction and mundane fiction, and a radical difference between
science fiction and magical fantasy.

In fiction, as I have pointed out, dreams and divina-
tory devices have a symbolic significance and an authority
which, in the real world, they lack. Mundane stories which
feature elaborately-symbolic dreams or prophetic oracles do
not necessarily tend towards the supernatural; the author's
motives for including them are usually to do with aesthetic
patterning, and they often have the status of ironic coincidences rather than metaphysical claims about the workability
of magic. The same is true of all the other symbolic devices
which stories routinely employ. In fantastic fiction, however,
matters of ironic coincidence are not so easily distinguished
from metaphysical claims, because the limits of possibility
are flexible. In magical fantasies and horror stories the supernatural is accepted at a fundamental level. This state of
affairs allows it to be taken for granted by the reader that
dreams and oracles are meaningful, because an acceptance of
magical connections between the visionary and the actual is
axiomatic to the contract between writer and reader.

Science fiction stories occupy a curious position
which is intermediate between those of mundane and supernatural fiction. In a science fiction story, the meaningfulness
of a dream or a prophecy can neither be immediately set
aside as a mere literary device, nor taken for granted as
something acceptable without further question. In science
fiction, if it is written with a good conscience and serious
intent, the question of how the dream or prophecy comes to
be meaningful ought to be asked and explored. Wherever
there are coincidences and connections between the events of
a sciencefictional narrative there ought to be an awkward
question raised as to whether—and if so, how—the connections are material. Science fiction is thus inexorably drawn
into speculation about the kinds of universe in which strange

things could happen, and the kinds of individuals who could do strange things.

Whenever science fiction is written with a good conscience, it cannot take matters of meaning for granted, one way or the other; it is always required to probe, to explore, to speculate, in a way that other genres are not. The climax of a good science fiction story is never a final closure of the specific questions which have been raised within it: the sense of wonder should always lead on to further questions, further investigations.

As in the case of contemporary moral philosophy, we frequently find modern philosophers who are interested in the problem of mind employing the vocabulary of science fiction to pose questions about the competence of various models of the mind, and about such notions as "identity" and "self-awareness." This is not surprising. Science-fictional ideas are necessary as instruments of this kind of philosophical investigation. Again, it is worth pointing out that in so far as it concerns itself with these kinds of questions, the science fiction genre—unlike the genre of Tolkienesque fantasy—is fundamentally at odds with the majority of dogmatic religions, which usually sidestep such questions by centralising some notion of an immortal soul whose properties are taken dogmatically for granted.

We must not forget that in spite of our sophisticated scientific understanding of the world at large, we are still very much a mystery to ourselves. We have competent working models of the universe, but not of our own inner selves. The private world of sensation and thought is very difficult to describe, and it has much in it which is strange and threatening: emotions, dreams, neurotic obsessions. If these exotic territories are properly to be explored, we cannot neglect the hard questions, which ask: if this were the case, what would it imply about the nature of mind, and the nature of reality. In getting to grips with such questions, science fiction is invaluable, and we should not underestimate the work which has been done by SF writers intent on exploring such notions as the possible nature of machine intelligence and the possible future evolution of the human mind.

The business of making up and telling stories is an aspect of human life whose importance can hardly be underestimated. It is by means of stories that we can best address, explore and familiarize ourselves with questions of moral order, and begin to investigate the enigmas of mind and matter. If we look at the nature and concerns of the earliest stories which we know about, this is manifestly obvious; it is only the great and confusing profusion of modern stories which has allowed it to become less than obvious. Science fiction is a recently-evolved instrument whose value in these respects should not be underestimated, and to which a great disservice is done by those who think of it only as one more kind of costume drama in which people run around fighting one another. Science fiction is essentially a kind of fiction in which people learn more about how to live in the real world, visiting imaginary worlds unlike our own in order to investigate by way of pleasurable thought-experiments how things might be done differently.

If we are to come to a proper understanding of the kind of beings we are, and the kind of universe we live in, and what opportunities we may have for shaping our place within that universe, we cannot do so without appropriate fictions. Many of those appropriate fictions do and will belong to the genre of science fiction, whose ideas and images are as significant in contemporary moral philosophy as they are in serious speculation about the future of human society. In a world which is changing as rapidly as ours is, we desperately need kinds of education which will make the imagination more flexible and more adaptable. Science fiction stories are, or could be, an invaluable resource in providing such an education. Only by paying serious attention to stories of this kind can people hope to improve their chances of learning to live in the strange and alien future world which the flow of actual events will precipitate out of the great spectrum of present possibility.

There is nothing intrinsically wrong with stories which deal only in ritual and repetition, as most popular genres do; such stories fulfil a valuable social and psychological function. But there is also work to be done by science fiction stories, which boldly go where other stories fear to tread.

The most valuable stories of all are surely those stories which aspire boldly to go where no other stories have ever been before, and which attempt, in their own particular fashion, to add to the heritage of our moral and imaginative wisdom.

III.

THE BRITISH AND AMERICAN TRADITIONS OF SPECULATIVE FICTION

What I want to do in this paper is compare and contrast the development of speculative fiction in two nations which share a common language. I have two purposes in mind in doing this. Firstly, I want to dramatize the sharp differences which existed at one time between the traditions of speculative fiction in Britain and America, but which have been partly obscured in much historical writing that lumps them together as aspects of a single story. Secondly, I want to suggest some explanations which help to account for these sharp differences.

It is, perhaps, surprising that early twentieth-century British speculative fiction, which I shall call for the sake of convenience "scientific romance," and early twentieth-century American speculative fiction, which I shall call "science fiction" were so strikingly different.[1] After all, many texts were published and read on both sides of the Atlantic, and the early SF magazines edited by Hugo Gernsback reprinted a good deal of work by the key figure in the British tradition, H. G. Wells. Nevertheless, despite this degree of shared access to one another's traditions, British writers and American writers were for several decades engaged in distinctly different projects, until scientific romance was engulfed by the tide of cultural "coca-colonization" which followed the end of World War II, and displaced by British science fiction.

Scientific romance became established as an identifiable popular genre during a boom in periodical publishing at the beginning of the 1890s. It had numerous historical connections with previously-existing genres, including Utopian fantasies and imaginary voyages, but two of these associations were of cardinal importance.

Scientific romance really grew out of the genre of future war stories which had been established in Britain in the wake of George Chesney's classic exercise in propaganda, *The Battle of Dorking* (1871). Two of the most important early writers of scientific romance, George Griffith and M. P. Shiel, achieved their first significant literary successes with future war stories, Griffith with *The Angel of the Revolution* and Shiel with *The Yellow Danger*. Many of the minor contributors to the genre, came into it by this route. H. G. Wells, the central figure of the tradition, wrote several important future war stories, including *The War in the Air* and "The Land Ironclads." Future war stories were to remain a vital component of scientific romance throughout its history, and might easily be regarded as the hard core of the genre.

In addition, the new genre was much enlivened by input drawn from the popular scientific journalism of the day, which abounded in speculative essays celebrating new discoveries in science and their possible implications. H. G. Wells began his literary career with such exercises in scientific journalism, and the imaginative premises used in his most famous scientific romances all emerged from flights of fantasy first couched in the form of essays—the gradual evolution of *The Time Machine* from an essay-like form to the story with which we are now familiar has been well-documented. Charles Howard Hinton, who published two volumes entitled *Scientific Romances* mingled therein essays and stories, while the French astronomer Camille Flammarion—a prolific writer of articles for the popular magazines—was one of the major influences on catastrophist fantasies of the day. This connection between scientific romance and speculative essays was also retained throughout the history of the genre.

The preoccupation with war exhibited by British speculative fiction of this period is easy to understand. As a tiny nation with a large worldwide empire inexorably in decline, Britain harbored a strong sense of threat, especially in respect of the imperialistic ambitions of the newly-consolidated German nation. Britons knew that they would eventually have to fight for their foreign possessions against other European nations, and the Great War was visible on the imaginative horizon for many years before it actually came. This anxiety was mixed with a determination to triumph, a desire to make permanently secure that which was under threat. Much future war fiction before 1914 was therefore belligerent and bloodthirsty. When the war did come, it arrived having been advertised for many years as a war that would end war, and Britons were all the more eager to fight it because of this pre-established mythology. The actual experience of the war, though, betrayed these expectations in no uncertain terms. It turned out to be the vilest of wars, horrific in its cost in human lives, which achieved nothing save the destruction of Europe as the economic heart of the world.

The writers of post-war scientific romance had to live with this betrayal of their hopes and dreams, and it is entirely understandable that their futuristic imagination thereafter focused in large measure on what they considered to be the historical lesson of the Great War: the belief that a new war, fought by air fleets which would bomb defenseless cities with high explosives and poison gas, would wreak destruction of a more horrific kind, and on a more terrible scale than was readily imaginable. Imagery of this kind features extensively in books like Edward Shanks's *People of the Ruins*, Cicely Hamilton's *Theodore Savage*, Neil Bell's *Gas War of 1940*, John Gloag's *Winter's Youth*, and S. Fowler Wright's trilogy, *Prelude in Prague*, *Four Days War*, and *Megiddo's Ridge*.

Americans, by contrast, felt themselves under no particular threat of invasion or involvement in war before 1914, and did not immediately involve themselves in the war in Europe. The historical situation of the U.S.A. was very different from Britain—it had, indeed, been the first great defector from the declining empire. Its geographical situation was just as obviously in complete contrast. The sheer size of the U.S.A., and the relative weakness of its neighboring na-

43

tions, made the idea that it might be invaded and overrun patently ridiculous.

Thus, the handful of future war stories produced in America before 1914 show not a trace of that desperate anxiety which fired the British genre. Because America came into the Great War late, and because it was so far away from the arenas of conflict, the effects of the war on the non-combatants at home were small by comparison with the effects of non-combatants in Europe. In effect, America became the only real winners of the war, when economic hegemony within the community of nations was shifted dramatically from devastated Europe to New York. The U.S.A. did suffer Depression after the Crash of 1929, but at that time Europe had still not recovered from 1918, and its plight was compounded by the Depression, becoming so much worse that the way was paved for the growth of Fascism, which ultimately precipitated the war of 1939.

Americans between the wars were largely, and understandably, untouched by the apocalyptic anxieties that fed and generated so much scientific romance: the fear of enemy air fleets obliterating civilization with poison gas simply did not seem applicable to the American situation. In consequence, American speculative fiction developed very differently. The American futuristic imagination was not constrained by that looming spectre of future war which kept its British counterpart in virtual captivity. Unfettered, American speculative writers took conspicuous advantage of certain opportunities almost entirely neglected by British writers. In particular, they became fascinated by interplanetary fantasies. A key figure in the development of the exotic romance which was eventually fed by pulp editors and writers into Hugo Gernsback's gadget-ridden "scientifiction" was Edgar Rice Burroughs, who used Mars and Venus as settings for marvellous adventurous odysseys which were, in essence, the ultimate daydreams.

This spirit of imaginative indulgence, though not at all consistent with Gernsback's manifesto for a futurological SF which would celebrate the liberating power of technological invention, infected science fiction to such a degree that hypothetical explorers were soon hurled beyond the bounds of the solar system in search of an infinite array of worlds where anything might exist and anything might happen. While scientific romance remained preoccupied with the dwindling and possible destruction of worldly empire, science fiction became entranced with the grandiose possibilities of galactic empire.

* * * * * * *

Scientific romance was continually enlivened, and thereby saved from being dour or imaginatively unambitious, by input from essays in speculative science. Wells, in his work in this vein, was carrying forward and strengthening a tradition which was as much intellectual play as anything else—a toying with ideas which was largely abstracted and amused; a variety of armchair philosophizing. After the Great War it extended through the works of such writers as J. B. S. Haldane and Julian Huxley, and spawned the extensive series of "Today & Tomorrow" pamphlets. Such cerebral ideative play fitted in well with the British *weltanschauung*.

In America, where ideative play was much more pragmatic and much more purposive, popular science writing tended to have a rather different emphasis, much more orientated toward tinkering with hardware. Where England prided itself on producing explorers, America was delighted to be the home of inventors, and the character of American speculative thought was geared to building gadgets rather than castles in the air. Thus, the way in which Hugo Gernsback asked his writers to borrow from science, and tried to derive scientifiction from the popular science journalism in which he had previously specialized, was different from the way science and scientific romance met and mingled. Gernsback's approval of and admiration for Wells should not blind us to the fact that the two men followed different imaginative procedures in quite distinctive styles.

The most imaginatively adventurous scientific romances—John Beresford's *The Hampdenshire Wonder*, E. V. Odle's *The Clockwork Man*, John Gloag's *Tomorrow's Yesterday*, and Murray Constantine's *Proud Man*[2] among them—tend to be rather dreamy works even when they are not, like Olaf Stapledon's *Star Maker* or John Beresford and Esmé Wynne-Tyson's *The Riddle of the Tower*, actual visionary fantasies. They frequently begin in country villages, and very often return full circle, with the initial circumstances restored, so that the world remains essentially undisturbed by the flight of fantasy. Science fiction novels very rarely do this: they often begin and almost always end with worlds radically transformed, altered out of all recognition, because their flights of fancy are very definitely incarnate, solidified in machinery and put into practice.

The pragmaticism of American speculative thought, contrasted with the abstractedness of British speculative thought, is not too difficult to understand when the historical situation of each nation is again considered. At the turn of the century the United States was a political and cultural entity still in the making, a civilization which was literally being built, raised out of the wilderness. Every new symbol of technological advance—the railroad, the oil well, the radio station—was contributing to a process of creation, and was seen in that light.

Britain, on the other hand, was a political and cultural entity based in long traditions, where change tended to be seen not in terms of creation, but in terms of disturbance and disruption. Its aristocracy had never been swept away, like the ancien regime in France, by a revolution: instead the traditional ruling class retained its prestige and cultural hegemony even though it was being gradually absorbed and usurped by the bourgeoisie and its nouveau riche. The writers of scientific romance were, almost without exception, champions of progress and apologists for new technology, but they had a thorough understanding of the fear of change and disruption that was part of their cultural heritage, and they fully appreciated how enormously difficult it would be to persuade their fellow Britons to accept change. H. G. Wells, perhaps the most eloquent and insistent propagandist for progress the nation produced, was continually forced, in both his fictional and non-fictional accounts of the shape of things to come, to suppose that the old order would have to be literally torn down or blasted apart before it could yield to a new.

America was freer than any other nation from the ideological legacy of an old order—freer even than revolutionary nations like France or Russia—because America had no traditional aristocracy which had owned its lands since the Middle Ages. Much of its territory, in fact, was effectively up for grabs. It was therefore wide open to American speculative writers to envisage the building of a radically new world, different from anything that had gone before. Britain, perhaps the least free of the developed nations from the burden of its past and the narcotization of conservatism, was at the opposite end of the ideological spectrum, despite its historical connections with the U.S.A. and their common language.

H. G. Wells dubbed the period following the end of the Great War "The Age of Frustration," and scientific romance between the wars can be regarded as an extraordinary elaboration of that spirit of frustration. It shows up not merely in the pessimistic fantasies of destruction by war, and in such cynical analyses of perverted Utopian dreams as Muriel Jaeger's *The Question Mark* and Aldous Huxley's *Brave New World*, but also in the supposedly optimistic works of the period. When hope for the future is offered in post-war scientific romance it is usually tied to the idea that there might be some kind of miraculous transcendence of the human condition—that a new race might appear free from the awful psychological hangups which prevent ordinary men from creating a just and satisfactory social order. Images of these "superior beings" can be found in the Amphibians of S. Fowler Wright's *The World Below*, the cat-people in John Gloag's *Tomorrow's Yesterday*, the Utopian supermen of John Beresford's "What Dreams May Come...?," the "Young Men" whose coming was celebrated in M. P. Shiel's last novel, the "elevator man" of Gerald Heard's *Doppelgängers*, and many of the future species in Olaf Stapledon's *Last and First Men*. Such superhumans are always contrasted with our own kind, and the reader of such books is invited—indeed, commanded—to feel humiliated and debased by comparison.

This quasi-nostalgic yearning to be replaced by something better, which reaches a literally hysterical pitch in

Claude Houghton's *This Was Ivor Trent*, and becomes the object of cunning black comedy in Andrew Marvell's *Minimum Man; or, Time to Be Gone*, contrasts very strongly with the use of superhumans in science fiction.

Early pulp supermen, like the one in John Taine's *Seeds of Life*, were usually menaces to be destroyed in the interests of preserving humanity. Later, science fiction writers followed the lead of A. E. van Vogt's *Slan* in seizing upon a notion popularized by J. B. Rhine's researches in ESP, that we all might be harboring latent superhuman powers just waiting for the right moment to come into bloom. Thus, while scientific romance was replete with images of exhausted, effete and decrepit humanity waiting to be overtaken, science fiction could present images of active, enthusiastic humanity equipped with new powers within as well as without—technological mastery combining with mental evolution to make certain that there could be no limits to human achievement. Very often in science fiction the reader is invited—indeed, commanded—to identify with the superman and feel proud of the identification.

Thus, in scientific romance of the thirties neither the future nor the stars could possibly belong to us, but only to those who might come after, while in science fiction of that era all of space and time was ours, to claim if we would. There is a sharp contrast to be drawn between the future of Olaf Stapledon's *Last and First Men* and the future of Laurence Manning's *The Man Who Awoke*, or between the universe of Stapledon's *Star Maker* and the universe of Isaac Asimov's Foundation series. In the scientific romances, the vast panorama of time and space is outside of the limited scope of our kind; in the science fiction stories, we are there: we come, we see, we conquer.

* * * * * * *

These ideological contrasts between scientific romance and science fiction are, of course, further complicated by contrasts in the relative stations of the two genres in the literary marketplace. The true fashionability of scientific romance lasted only as long as the experimental phase of the middlebrow popular fiction magazines—they had virtually abandoned their enthusiastic championship of *outré* material as early as 1905. From then on scientific romance was considered esoteric, and was effectively forced to seek a place in more rarefied strata of the market—it filled a spectrum extending from the cheerfully middlebrow to the earnestly highbrow; its imaginatively adventurous works became increasingly heavy in their philosophical pretensions, to the point where the paperback reprint of *Last and First Men* was a Pelican book packaged as though it were non-fiction.

In America, by contrast, science fiction was caught up in a kind of fictional brand warfare when the popular pulp magazines began genre specialization as a marketing tactic. Speculative fiction was gradually squeezed out of the middlebrow magazines as they began to cultivate different images in consequence of the kind of advertising they were carrying. The spectrum of American science fiction thus extended from precariously middlebrow outlets like John Campbell's *Astounding* to unashamedly lowbrow pulps featuring costume drama and adventure stories of a kind relegated in Britain to the boys' papers.

Because of these contrasting developments in the fiction markets in Britain and the U.S.A., scientific romance remained much more closely in touch with customary criteria of literary merit than science fiction did, until the end of World War II, when science fiction's rapid sophistication coincided with its massive penetration of the British popular fiction market. Ironically, it was in the same post-war decade that a good deal of British speculative fiction began to appear in the lowbrow regions of the market via cheap paperback books (though by that time the "science fiction" label had ben imported and much of the fiction was produced in imitation of American pulp SF).

The relative literary sophistication of much scientific romance will inevitably encourage literary critics to see it as a superior genre to contemporary pulp SF, and perhaps to regret its absorption, in the 1950s, into a generalized Anglo-American popular culture. This should not allow us, however, to overlook the fact that both genres had their particular merits and virtues.

The virtues of scientific romance were its moral earnestness, its anxious concern with possible abuses of technology, its scrupulous scepticism regarding the mythology of progress and its corollary analyses of the many ways in which ideals of freedom and justice might be subverted.

The virtues of early science fiction were its imaginative ambition and enthusiasm, its prolific inventiveness and melodramatic grandiosity, its hunger for ingenious novelties and its corollary fecundity of images and ideas.

There is an ironic sense in which what each genre tended to lack was exactly what the other had in abundance, and the rapid convergent evolution of the two genres after World War II can thus be seen as a kind of productive cross-fertilization and as an advantageous blending of interests. The revitalized post-World War II science fiction of America and Britain is a healthier and more admirable genre than its pulp predecessor or scientific romance.

I think, however, that we should be prepared to see more in the merging of science fiction and scientific romance than simply a fusion of marketplaces. We should also recognize that the elements of contrast between the cultural backgrounds which generated such different species of speculative fiction have to some extent been overtaken by events.

The sense of threat and apocalyptic anxiety, which generated so many fantasies of world destruction in Britain while America remained complacent, is now no longer confined to Europe. America is no longer beyond the potential reach of the forces of destruction. Although World War II did not, as so many British speculators feared, obliterate civilization in Europe—largely because the Geneva Convention held up far better than anyone expected it to—it did, in the manner of its closure, introduce the world to a new apocalyptic threat: the atom bomb. When Russia began testing nuclear weapons America was infected for the first time with a kind of fear and a sense of threat which had been endemic in Europe for decades. The anxiety-level of American science fiction was thus stepped up by an important order of magnitude which brought its world-view much more closely into line with that of scientific romance.

In addition to this, the expansive phase of American development was slowly petering out. The U.S.A. stopped importing legions of European immigrants, and began instead to consolidate. The western frontier disappeared, swallowed up by the sheer munificence of the success of its pioneers. New transport and communications systems contributed to a metaphorical shrinking of the vast nation. America had inherited a kind of ideological empire by virtue of its exploits in World War II, but then saw that empire go into the kind of rebellious decline which had earlier overtaken the British Empire. Inevitably, America saw in the decades following World War II the growth of exactly that kind of conservative spirit which Britain had inherited from its historical tradition, and American speculative writers quickly came to understand, even if they did not sympathize with, the characterization of change as disturbance and disruption rather than progress and opportunity.

In the 1950s, therefore, American science fiction had little option but to take on board many of the features of scientific romance, and by so doing make the continuance of an independent tradition of scientific romance redundant. After World War II Britain and America have come to share, in very large measure, a commonwealth of outlook, experience and anxiety which makes the speculative fiction produced in the two nations much more similar in its tone and concerns than could have been the case between 1890 and 1945.

In spite of this conflation of the two traditions, though, I think it is still possible to find in British science fiction a distinctive kind of flavor. Much of it still retains a kind of cool sobriety which can be contrasted with the heat and hyperactivity of much American SF. When British SF is nostalgic, as it often is, it is nostalgic in a rather pastoral vein. Some American SF is nostalgic like that, too, but much of it is nostalgic in a very different way, looking backward precisely when it pretends to be most forward-looking, hoping to rediscover somewhere outside the earth a new frontier where all the old pulpish dreams will once more become meaningful. The assertive pragmaticism of old is still retained by much American SF, often becoming more propagandist in the face of assumed unfashionability. In contrast, that fanciful abstracted pipedreaming which played so large a part in inspiring scientific romance still lies at the root of much British SF, which tends to view assertive pragmaticism as a kind of vulgar clowning. The champions of change in British SF still tend to stand back from their images of evolutionary transcendence, while much American SF still yearns for the incipient superhumanity of the man in the street. In these respects there is still a sense in which British and American speculative fiction are divided within their commonwealth, using the same vocabulary of ideas but speaking with distinctive accents.

IV.

THE BIOLOGY AND SOCIOLOGY OF ALIEN WORLDS

In 1901, the first year of the twentieth century, George Griffith published *A Honeymoon in Space*, a novel in which the Earl of Redgrave invents a fabulous flying machine, the Astronef, which he uses first to put a stop to war, and then to take his new American bride on a tour of the solar system.

Their first port of call is the moon, which they find to be an old, dead world, where air and water are to be found only in deep chasms. The cities of the moon have been in ruins for an incalculable time, and the last survivors of the humanoid race which built them have degenerated to bestiality in the depths of the dark abysses.

They find that Mars too is an older world than Earth, whose inhabitants have "passed the zenith of civilization and are dropping back into savagery." Their cities are grouped along the equator, supplied with water by great networks of canals. The Martians are, of course, humanoid, but have "civilized themselves out of all emotions," and have been brought to a fierce savagery by the ruthless struggle for existence which has attended the decline of their world.

Venus, by contrast, they discover to be inhabited by ethereal winged people, like angels or the delicate fairies of Victorian art. These people make their visitors welcome—unlike the men of Mars, who attacked without warning—and are utterly without sin. Redgrave and his wife are tempted to remain with them, but fear that their influence might be corrupting; although they are as virtuous and high-minded a pair as Earth can produce they nevertheless carry the stain of original sin within their humanity.

Jupiter turns out to be a violent world still in the throes of its creation, and not yet an abode of life. On its satellite Ganymede, however, the honeymooners find a people so technologically advanced as to be able to take control of the Astronef. Luckily, they mean their visitors no harm, being men like gods—or, at least, like demigods, handsome and powerful. They remind Lord Redgrave strongly of what he has read in a book called *The End of the World*, by the French astronomer Camille Flammarion, where Flammarion presented a vision of the ultimate products of human progress.

From the crystal cities of Ganymede the voyagers go on to Saturn, whose thick atmosphere supports a life-system of its own, inhabited by gigantic aerial jellyfish and other strange creatures on which they prey. The honeymoon is then cut short following an unforeseen and near-disastrous encounter with a dark star in the outer fringes of the solar system.

A Honeymoon in Space is interesting because it brings together into a somewhat ill-mixed assembly many of the ideas which speculative writers of its time had concerning life on other worlds. It was not the first account of interplanetary tourism by any means, but it was one of the first in which the scientific imagination came to outweigh religious imagination as a source of inspiration. Many earlier writers had proposed that the other worlds in the universe must have been populated by God just as ours was, and had given descriptions of life on those worlds. They had represented the intelligent inhabitants of other worlds, almost without exception, as people very like ourselves—made, of course, in God's own image. They had also, for the most part, represented the inhabitants of other planets as more virtuous people than the denizens of Earth, in order to show their readers what heights of spiritual perfection might be possible if only we could find the moral will to scale them.

There is, of course, a strong vein of this kind of thinking in Griffith's novel. He does not hesitate to populate Venus with angelic and sinless beings, and to contrast their lot with our own. There are other influences operating upon him, though, which are equally noticeable. There is an assumption borrowed from nineteenth-century anthropological evolutionists, that all possible societies might be seen as stages in a long progress from barbarism to civilization, to be followed by a regress to degeneracy. His images of alien life are located, along with contemporary human societies, on a scale that resembles the life-cycle of an individual person. There is also, less obviously, the influence of Darwin's biological evolutionism, to be found in references to the struggle for existence which has shaped the nature of the decadent Martians, and provided Saturn with an alien life-system adapted to the strange conditions presumed to exist there. Had Griffith read his Flammarion more attentively, or even his Wells, he might have done much more in this line, but he was content with the easier assumption that for the most part aliens could be represented simply as slightly-modified people.

Nowadays, of course, science fiction writers are much more conscientious and much more knowledgeable. We know now that none of the other worlds in the solar system could support humanoid life. We know that the canals of Mars were an illusion, and we know how silly it is blithely to assume that the atmospheres of alien worlds are like our own. We have given much more careful consideration to the problems that might arise in a hypothetical first contact with aliens. Unlike Griffith, we do not assume that the aliens would probably be able to speak English, or at the very worst would be able to communicate with the aid of the kind of sign-language which might suffice to carry an Englishman through a Thomas Cook tour of Egypt. By comparison with *A Honeymoon in Space*, modern science fiction is highly sophisticated.

On the other hand, one can find some intriguing parallels between Griffith's story and many more recent works of scientific romance. There is a sense, indeed, in which the similarities between *A Honeymoon in Space* and some contemporary works are more interesting than the differences. It may even be arguable that the pattern of development of modern science fiction has doubled back on itself, so that the concerns of present-day novels describing alien societies are actually closer to those of Griffith's novel than were works published between the two world wars.

Nobody reads George Griffith any more. Even in his own time his reputation as a writer of scientific romance was quite eclipsed by the fame won by his contemporary, H. G. Wells. By 1901 Wells had already offered his own account of man's possible future evolution in *The Time Machine*, and had presented some authentically alien beings in *The War of the Worlds*. Wells's science fiction was determinedly secular in character, and although he had described an angel's visit to Earth in *The Wonderful Visit*, he certainly would never have been guilty of populating an alien world with such individuals. Though he was to deal with the substance of religious mythology in numerous later works Wells had no doubt that in designing alien life-forms it was to biological science, and especially to Darwinian evolutionary theory, that one must look for guidance. In the same year that Griffith produced *A Honeymoon in Space*, Wells produced *The First Men in the Moon*, the first conscientious attempt to provide a thorough description of an alien society and its ways.

In *The First Men in the Moon* the scientist Cavor is marooned among the Selenites, who live deep below the lunar surface, and is able to transmit back to Earth some messages describing their way of life. The Selenites are emphatically unhuman, being insectile in general appearance and socially organized after the fashion of an Earthly beehive.

The central assumptions of Wells's fiction about aliens were taken up by a host of writers of interplanetary melodrama. It became commonplace to assume that the inhabitants of other worlds would be monstrous creatures, resembling giant versions of loathsome Earthly creatures, or strange chimerical hybrids. Their attitude to human beings would be hostile—often they would appear in the role of would-be invaders of Earth, greedy to exploit such a succulent world. It became commonplace, too, to adopt as a model for alien social organization the most obvious example which life on Earth offered: the hive organization of the social insects.

Monstrous aliens dominated American pulp science fiction from the time of its first appearance until the end of the 1930s. The representation of alien life in this period was primarily an exercise in teratology. There were humanoid aliens too, and sometimes there were nice non-human aliens who resembled lovable Earthly creatures like birds or teddy bears, but for the most part aliens were frightful creatures, who had to be wiped out before they exterminated us. Largely because of the acquisition of this image, other writers tended to leave aliens alone. Even the use of other-worldly societies as satirical mirrors of our own—whose distinguished tradition extended back to the eighteenth century—fell temporarily into disfavor.

The attempt by a group of writers connected with the magazine *Astounding Science Fiction* to introduce a new realism into American science fiction helped to transform stories of alien life in the 1940s and 1950s. A few writers began to pay more serious attention to the business of designing coherent and fairly complicated life-systems to fit the physical environments of other worlds. Writers like Hal Clement and Poul Anderson eventually developed a considerable skill at this particular imaginative game. Although producers of science fiction vary considerably in terms of the skill and the conscientiousness which they bring to the business of designing alien biospheres, it is probably fair to say that nowadays the job is often done well.

This progress toward a more sensible and sophisticated use of biological science in presenting alien life-forms has coincided with a similar progress in the use of anthropological science. There is, of course, a certain falseness in using analyses of unusual human societies as a source of inspiration for the modelling of alien societies, but when it is done cleverly this can be very effective. Since the 1950s, in fact, many writers have used stories of encounters between humans and aliens to construct fables relevant to the way that human societies see one another and treat one another. There have been some particularly powerful attacks on the politics of colonialism, best exemplified by Ursula K. Le Guin's short novel, *The Word for World Is Forest*. Other recent examples of sophisticated pseudo-anthropological SF include Michael Bishop's *Transfigurations* and Philip Mann's *The Eye of the Queen*.

There is nothing very surprising about this pattern of change. Once there was pressure upon writers to attempt to be more realistic in constructing hypothetical worlds it was inevitable that the shallowness and silliness of writers like Griffith would be left far behind. Of course, the cinema, dealing to a far greater extent in gaudy visual imagery and far less in detailed exposition, did not follow suit. Monster movies dominated SF films until well into the 1960s, and even now compete on almost level terms with a gentler and sicklier brand of extra-terrestrials. Film makers are quite prepared to design bizarre costumes for human actors to wear or weird models for puppeteers to animate, but the job of designing an appropriate alien environment around them would probably be too much for even the most liberal budget to bear.

Even in the world of the printed word, though, the trend toward greater realism in the presentation of alien worlds and alien societies is not the only pattern that can be seen, nor is it really the most interesting one. Something else rather more peculiar has happened, which is that after a period of time when the religious themes which still echo in *A Honeymoon in Space* were deliberately rejected, they have crept back in again and have gained steadily in prominence and importance. Science fiction, which was once a determinedly secular species of fantasy, has reimported several different kinds of mysticism, overt and covert.

The potential which the vocabulary of ideas developed by the SF writers offered for religious allegory was seen in the 1940s by C. S. Lewis, who exploited it in his novels *Out of the Silent Planet* and *Perelandra*. By the 1950s several writers working for the American SF magazines had begun to select premises from Christian theology for exploration in the logical manner favored by the genre. Examples include Ray Bradbury's "The Fire Balloons" and James Blish's *A Case of Conscience*, both of which required the invention of alien races, and the latter involving the invention of a whole life-system.

Closely linked to these exercises in speculative theology are a number of stories which use imaginary biology to provide analogues of religious ideas. Clifford Simak's novel *Time and Again* imagines alien commensals which exist undetected in all living beings: science-fictional versions of the soul. George R. R. Martin's story "A Song for Lya" imagines an alien creature which can absorb the living brains of sentient creatures, taking their minds into itself and assuring them of a kind of immortality. Robert Silverberg's novel *Downward to the Earth* is a story of alien beings whose religion promises them redemption and rebirth, and whose biology makes this literally possible, not only for them but for a human who adopts their ways.

One of the most striking correlates of this remystification of science fiction has been the dramatic change which has overtaken stories about alien hive-minds. Early stories of hive-societies almost invariably follow Wells in representing such a state as an horrific one. John Beresford and Esmé Wynne-Tyson's novel *The Riddle of the Tower* is a powerful cautionary tale expressing the anxiety that the human race might be evolving toward a hive state. David H. Keller's early pulp SF novel, *The Human Termites*, in a crude and highly lurid manner, gives voice to a similar anxiety in describing a parapsychological power grab by alien intelligences. In the 1950s the alien "bugs" in Robert Heinlein's *Starship Troopers* are represented as the ultimate enemy of mankind, who must not only be defeated but exterminated, because their intelligent hive-society cannot possibly co-exist with humankind.

Even in the 1950s, however, a different outlook could be seen in other works. While for some writers hive-society remained the ultimate totalitarianism, opposed to all the values associated with individualism and freedom which we hold so dear, for others it became the symbol of a supernatural kinship, a loving union which could dispel loneliness and human alienation. Thus, in Theodore Sturgeon's novella "To Marry Medusa" (expanded to book length as *The Cosmic Rape*), the attempt by a vast alien hive-mind to absorb humankind into itself goes perversely wrong as the connection of human minds into a collective intelligence produces a benign being so powerful that it is the invader which is absorbed, tamed and transformed. In the last quarter of a century hive-minds have had a much better press in science fiction, and although they are still sometimes represented in horrific terms, they are frequently described sympathetically, and often considered to embody moral and spiritual lessons that mankind would do well to learn. Even when they remain implacably alien, as in Joe Haldeman's *The Forever War*, they are subjected to more scrupulous analysis.

This shift in emphasis from the representation of hive societies as the perfection of tyranny to consideration of hive organization as a quasi-supernatural kind of social harmony is the tip of an iceberg. One can find much more widely distributed within sciencefictional images of alien life a powerful fascination with the idea of harmony in nature as the means to achieving harmony in social affairs. Like certain political movements in Europe and America, many science fiction writers have seized upon the word "ecology," which has for them acquired an almost talismanic significance.

In the context of biological science, ecology is of course simply a field of study; it is the study of organisms in relation to their environment, and necessarily involves consideration of the complex relationships between different species living in the same locality. Clearly, the study of man in relation to his many natural environments is one which has many practical connotations, and it is therefore not surprising that ecological matters have come into the arena of political discussion and decision. Perhaps it is not surprising either that most members of the general public have only the vaguest notion of what ecological science is all about and what kind of issues are really at stake. What is a little surprising, however, is the extent to which ecological concerns and ecological terminology have become, in popular rhetoric at least, saturated with a peculiar mysticism. Nowhere is this mysticism more obvious and more extensively developed than in the mythology of contemporary science fiction.

It is quite commonplace today to hear people discoursing on the need for people to "live in harmony with nature" instead of "opposing" it. Usually they have only the vaguest idea what they might mean by this, but the argument seems to rest on the assumption that there is some kind of essential balance in nature which modern technological societies have violated. I use the word "violated" deliberately, to try to capture the sense in which this argument is meant: there is an underlying claim to the effect that what we have done constitutes some kind of sin; that we have in some mysterious sense fallen from ecological grace. The political programmes associated with ecological concerns frequently advise us not only to order our affairs more sensibly, but also to cultivate a kind of special reverence for "Nature" which amounts occasionally even to a form of worship. This kind of ecological religiosity can be clearly seen, for instance, in Ernest Callenbach's recent novel of Utopian political planning, *Ecotopia*, which has a cult following in America.

One can find an extraordinarily powerful example of ecological religiosity in a strange novel by the nineteenth-century naturalist W. H. Hudson, *A Crystal Age*, published in 1887, but for more than half a century after the publication of that novel it remained unique. In the last twenty years, though, many science fiction novels have been published which recover something of its spirit. The first of them may have been Mark Clifton's novel *Eight Keys to Eden*, one of many novels about the colonization of alien worlds in which the colonists find an enigmatic Arcadian world, lush with Earthlike life but which pose unexpected problems of adaptation.

The myth of the Garden of Eden has become one of the most frequent referents in stories of men on alien but Earthlike worlds. The process of adapting to such worlds is very often represented in terms of forging a new relationship with a new ecosphere, which must be crucially different from the old one. There will be, or at least should be, a re-harmonization of man and nature—a reversal of the fall from ecological grace which is presumed, tacitly, to have happened on Earth. We find something of this in the memorable climax of Ray Bradbury's *Martian Chronicles*, but it is much more pronounced in more recent works where forests come to have the same mesmeric fascination as they do in Hudson's *A Crystal Age* and Callenbach's *Ecotopia*. We can find it in works by Ursula K. Le Guin and Michael G. Coney which appear to be primarily political fantasies, and more obviously in novels like Neil Barrett's *Highwood*, John Brunner's *Bedlam Planet*, Gordon Dickson's *Masters of Everon*, and Sydney Van Scyoc's *Sunwaifs*. These explicit examples are all minor works, but one can find extensions of the mode of thinking into much more famous novels whose full range of concerns is much more elaborate: ecological mysticism is part and parcel of the more general mysticism of the works of Frank Herbert, seen both in his Dune novels and his striking hive-mind stories *The Green Brain* and *Hellstrom's Hive*.

This frequent crediting of alien life-systems with a supernatural harmony is reflected in the characteristic portrayal of sentient alien beings, who are nowadays frequently represented neither as savage monsters nor as human beings in funny costumes, but as beings who have found an existential peace denied to tormented and alienated humans. Alien beings have not only become lovable, but also admirable: they are better men than we are. This, at least, is something that the cinema can convey in its particular limited way, and both *Close Encounters of the Third Kind* and *E.T.* have mined this new vein of potential sympathy and reverence. The mysticism, magicality and religiosity of both films is striking.

This recent trend means that when we look back today at such novels as *A Honeymoon in Space*, we find that those aspects of it which seemed to be the last dying echoes of an old tradition—particularly the representation of the inhabitants of Venus—actually have obvious analogies with the feelings and ideas in many contemporary accounts of human encounters with alien worlds and alien beings. The specifically Christian references may have been replaced with something which, in terms of the history of religions, may seem more basic or more primitive, but the essential imaginative enterprise is not dissimilar.

What conclusion, then, should we draw from these observations? One inference that one might take is that the supposed realism of much modern science fiction—its claim to be concerned with the rational extrapolation of hypotheses whose inspiration comes from the progress of scientific knowledge—is a sham. Even in the work of some very competent and realistic writers—for instance Poul Anderson, whose handling of alien life-systems is as conscientious as any—one can nevertheless see these other things going on.

This is, however, only one way of looking at the issue and not necessarily the most appropriate one. One might instead take the inference that this metaphysical current within contemporary SF reveals by its very power and dubious propriety something about the nature of the contemporary popular imagination. It seems that an attempt to purge speculative endeavor of metaphysical concerns—a project which parallels in its own fashion the attempt by the positivist philosophers to purge science of metaphysical pollution—has been made, and has failed. An attempt to confine or delimit an area of speculative adventure to worldly possibilities and purely materialistic concerns has been made and has come unstuck, not because the project was impossible, but for the far more serious reason that it proved to be uninteresting. Metaphysical issues and disguised religiosity crept back, not because they were necessary in some absolute sense, but because they carried with them a certain fascination which animates the stories whose imaginative territory they have reoccupied, makes them more vivid, and gives them an appearance of profundity which they otherwise could not present.

Ecological mysticism and sciencefictional religiosity are, in one sense, a sham. They represent one of the ways in which the supposed responsibility of science fiction to actual science is a mere pretence. Their presence in modern SF should not, however, be regarded simply as a failure of that fiction to live up to its own ideals, or as evidence of crassness on the part of the writers working within the genre. It would, in fact, be naive to think that attempts by science fiction writers to represent alien life-systems and alien societies are actually thought-experiments in speculative biology and speculative sociology. They are not, though there is a certain utility in pretending that they are.

The interest of writers and readers in representations of alien life and representations of alien society is not, in fact, much like the interest of the biologist in Earthly life or the interest of the anthropologist in Earthly societies. We are interested in such imaginative constructions not for their own sake, nor for the competence with which they build upon what we know about biology or social science, but because they are instruments we can use to think and talk about ourselves. They embody opinions we have about ourselves, about the way we are and about the ways we might be. We must expect, therefore, our images of alien biology and alien sociology to embody the various ideas which people already have and routinely use in talking and thinking about mankind and about our existential predicament. Given this, it would be peculiar indeed if metaphysical and theological speculation were absent from contemporary science fiction, and their presence is evidence of its determination to make a serious claim upon the attention of readers rather than evidence of the failure of its own prospectus.

V.

COSMIC PERSPECTIVES IN NINETEENTH-CENTURY LITERATURE

In his preface to *Eureka*, which is variously subtitled "A Prose Poem" or "An Essay on the Material and Spiritual Universe," Edgar Allan Poe offers us a "book of truths," but requests us to judge it "as a poem only." He suggests, for the benefit of those who think the term "poem" unsuitable, that the word "romance" might also describe it, and as I prefer the latter term I shall accept his invitation, but what I want to do, in essence, is what Poe asks me to do; I shall consider *Eureka* as a romance, and will attempt to say something about the kind of romance it is by examining its nature, its sources of inspiration and its resemblances to other works of the same sub-genre, particularly to Camille Flammarion's *Stories of Infinity*.

Eureka was published in 1848—Europe's "year of revolutions" and it claims to attempt something revolutionary: a survey of the universe. By "universe" here Poe means something more than the mere physical universe, which he calls "the universe of stars." He wants to extend what is known about that lesser universe, thanks to astronomical science, by means of a "mental gyration" which will penetrate the metaphysical reality included and implied by what is actually observable.

Poe is scornful of the positivism which seeks to exclude such metaphysical speculations and intuitions from the realm of knowledge, and expresses his scorn in a satirical essay borrowed from his story "Mellonta Tauta," which pretends to have been written in the year 2848. From this advanced viewpoint the essayist condemns the deductive and inductive approaches to enlightenment, here credited to "Aries Tottle" (Aristotle) and "Hog" (Francis Bacon), which are championed in John Stuart Mill's *System of Logic*. These are condemned as "narrow and crooked paths, the one of creeping and the other of crawling," and it is claimed that the true road to enlightenment overleaps these. The essayist calls it "the majestic highway of the Consistent," and by it he means a kind of speculative intuition which imagines theories whole and coherent, and embodies a conviction based in the beautiful consistency of the whole. This intuition, he concedes, may be reckoned a form of guesswork, but should not be derided as unfounded or irrational on that account—it is the process he finds at work in the thinking of such great men of science as Kepler and Laplace.

The image of the universe which Poe then develops is in part an extrapolation of ideas embodied in the dialogue which forms the main part of his story "A Mesmeric Revelation" (1844). There the mesmerized man, in a state of suspended animation, is sufficiently isolated from sensory input to achieve a marvellously heightened perception of the true state of things. He is able to comprehend that God is the "ultimate or unparticled matter" which permeates and impels everything; that He is the Universal Mind whose thoughts are the objects of Creation. Death is not extinction but rather a process of metamorphosis, by which the individual acquires a new body, too refined to be capable of sensory detection, and yet still an incarnation which preserves individuality against dissolution in the formless spirit of the God-Mind. Ultimate life is thus "un-organ-ized," organic life being a fleshly cage whose bars to perception are only feebly penetrated by the organs of sense; all the matter in the universe exists to supply "pabulum" for the organs of the "rudimental beings" which inhabit the countless worlds of the stars. Organic life, unlike life-after-death, permits pain, and pain exists to give meaning, by contrast, to pleasure—to the "bliss of the ultimate life in heaven."

Eureka does not have quite the same visionary ambition and extravagance of this. It does talk about the nature of

God, in much the same pantheistic terms (though Poe disliked and disowned the term "pantheism"), but in more pseudoscientific terms. Creation here becomes the willing into being of the "primordial particle"; the universe is organized by the balance and interplay of the opposed forces of attraction and repulsion, which are manifest in gravity and electricity, and in body and soul. Contemplation of the mysteries of gravity and electromagnetism gives rise to "soul-reveries" which warrant this extension of metaphors.

Eureka then goes on to discuss at some length, and in some detail, Laplace's Nebular Hypothesis of the origin of the solar system, and various related matters. Poe argues that John Herschel's revelation that some nebulae are collections of stars does not falsify the Laplace theory, but simply suggests that these nebulae are very distant star-systems like our own galaxy. He tries hard to convey to his reader some sense of the true magnitude of cosmic distances as revealed by the observations of Bessel and Struve (who had recently—in 1838—measured the parallax of two of the nearer stars). He also wades into another controversy of the astronomy of the day, regarding the question of whether the visible stars revolve around a great central sun; he attacks Mädler for asserting that they do (though he may have mistaken Mädler's actual position).

These passages, which strongly resemble more recent exercises in the popularization of science, are interwoven with metaphysical extrapolations, rhapsodizing about the idea of the infinite; hypothesizing that there might be an infinity of universes, each one "in the bosom" of its own God; and finally looking forward to the ultimate destiny of our universe, when matter has re-achieved "unity" (a notion which must seem to modern readers a curious anticipation of the entropic heat-death which more recent theories point to). Even here Poe wants to reach further still, and suggests that this achievement of unity might be followed by a new Creation, part of an eternal sequence: the pulsation of the "Heart Divine," which is by some ultimate analogy also the beating of our own hearts. By "heart" Poe probably means to imply more than the obvious analogy; Vincent Buranelli points out that he was influenced considerably by Pascal, whose famous dictum that "the heart has its reasons which the reason knows not" means by "heart" a kind of apprehension very similar to Poe's "intuition."[1]

The modern reader may find it surprising that Poe asks us to consider this treatise in speculative metaphysics, which seems so solidly embedded in astronomical science, as a romance. It may seem that this is a defensive move—a cowardly attempt to duck the necessity of rational defense. But we need to bear in mind some cautionary notes. The separation between "literary" modes of discourse and what we would now call a "scientific paper" was still in the process of being made in 1848. The first specialized scientific journal only appeared in 1800—as a public correspondence between astronomers, who were the first scientists to organize themselves into an international community with some degree of organized co-operation. Scientific and philosophical discourse had not entirely abandoned such forms as the dialogue, and it was of course open to a writer like Poe to present a work of fiction (like "A Mesmeric Revelation") as if it were a piece of reportage, or to embed an essay, elaborately decked with literary jokes, in a fantasy (as he does in "Mellonta Tauta"). In asking whether *Eureka* is a literary work or a treatise—fiction or non-fiction—we would be wrong to require that it must be one thing or the other; the principle of the excluded middle is one of the things Poe satirizes in his joke at Aristotle's expense.

The combination of treatise and fantasy, in curious amalgam, is even more marked in some of the works that resemble *Eureka* most closely, the cardinal examples being certain works of the French astronomer Camille Flammarion: the *Stories of Infinity*, one of which—*Lumen*—was later expanded to book length; *Urania*; and *Omega: The Last Days of the World*. Flammarion was more intimately involved in the development of astronomical science than Poe, and was more competent to assess its theories by virtue of his privilege in living through a period when many more discoveries were made. His status as a man of science, though, did not prevent his extrapolating a metaphysical system to contain and dramatize his scientific data, adopting ideas about the life-after-death of the disembodied soul and the incarnation of souls in alien life-forms on many different worlds which strongly recall passages in "A Mesmeric Revelation" (though a more obvious inspiration of and model for *Lumen* is Fontenelle's classic *Plurality of Worlds*).

Later works which contain echoes of the cosmic perspectives of *Eureka* are more obviously works of fiction: Wells's "Under the Knife" and Hodgson's *House on the Borderland* are obviously romances, though they contain visions which do try to communicate a sense of the true scale of the universe. The most extravagant twentieth-century exercise in this vein—Olaf Stapledon's *Star Maker*—is an obvious amalgam of essay and fiction, but remains much closer to the mode of story-telling than the manner of scientific treatise. Where there are echoes of *Eureka* in modern science fiction—and one can find them in the works of writers as various as A. E. van Vogt[2] and Charles Sheffield[3]—the authors do make some claim to intellectual seriousness, but are clearly operating as novelists. The steady movement of such speculative works toward the appearance of fiction, however, should not be allowed to make us forget their common cause with *Eureka*: their purpose is to say something about the size and scale and nature of the universe to which we supposedly should attend, and from which we might gain some kind of emotional or spiritual uplift. Their romance is of a special kind: it attempts to awake a sense of wonder, and by that awakening seeks to impart to us something of the moral conviction which grips those who travel "the majestic highway of the Consistent."

Poe's epistemology—his notion of the role of the imagination in science—is of course dubious, although it is worth noting that the manner in which Kepler arrived at his hypotheses has also come in for close scrutiny by modern philosophers of science like Norwood Hanson. Whether aesthetic considerations really do have a role to play in our judgments of what is true is a question that can be left aside. What is more to the point here is the indubitable fact that scientific discoveries do have aesthetic consequences; their revelations certainly stimulate the imagination in a way that can readily be analogized to the stimulus of poetry. The Scottish poet William Wilson, who coined the term "Science-Fiction" in 1851, defined this nascent genre in terms of "the Poetry of Science." "The Study and extraction of Poetry from these sciences," he wrote, "is like reading mighty books of Life, Beauty and Divinity." The Man of Science, he observes, "knows that neither Matter nor Mind ever die; and that if the fixed laws of Attraction and Repulsion were for one instant disturbed, the whole physical Creation would fall back that moment into Chaos."[4]

The science of astronomy lends itself particularly well to this kind of imaginative stimulation. The new and more powerful telescopes which were constructed in the early nineteenth century—like John Herschel's instrument at the Cape of Good Hope—extended the reach of human eyesight further and further into the universe, and a whole series of new techniques brought further insights into its nature: Fraunhofer's mapping of the solar spectrum; Herschel's pioneering work in photometry. Another astronomer who was also a writer of proto-science fiction, Garrett P. Serviss, observed in the Preface to his book *Curiosities of the Sky* that "What Froude says of history is true also of astronomy: it is the most impressive where it transcends explanation.... The dominion which astronomy has always held over the minds of men is akin to that of poetry; when the former becomes merely instructive and the latter purely didactic, both lose their power over the imagination."[5]

It was this aesthetic dimension of astronomy which attracted Camille Flammarion to its study, which encouraged him to devote so much effort to the popularization of the science, and which encouraged him to take off from his observations into such flights of fancy as the "History of a Comet," in which Halley's Comet communicates its observations of the history of the Earth and mankind as glimpsed during its many passages of the planet's orbit. Flammarion's ability to draw striking images out of astronomical discoveries made him a frequent contributor to the popular magazines of the late nineteenth century, when his articles often appeared with bold illustrations of hypothetical comets striking the Earth and other such apocalyptic events. It was Flammarion more than any other writer who popularized images of alien life: inhabitants of other worlds adapted to very different physical conditions. His works frequently echo Poe's, particularly the imagery of the "Mesmeric Revelation," and he took very seriously the supposed revelations about life on other worlds communicated to him by spiritualist mediums. In *Urania* he uses the device of messages received in a hypnotic trance to confirm and extend insights which the character George Spero has already intuited on the basis of his scientific researches. The rhetoric of Flammarion and Poe is strikingly similar, though their jargon differs, so that where Poe speaks of the Heart Divine, Flammarion's Spero refers to God the "universal soul," and where Poe's mesmerized man discourses on unparticulate matter, Spero rhapsodizes about "Force."

It seems very likely that Flammarion had read Poe's work in this vein—his "In Infinity" involves an account of deciphering an enigmatic message which is surely inspired by Poe's story "The Gold Bug"—but what we see here is not copying but a near-identical process of inspiration. Like Poe, Flammarion is prepared to assert that a truthful vision of the nature of the universe has an intrinsic poetic quality. In the dialogue *Lumen*, the longest of the *Stories of Infinity*, the questioning student regrets that the heavens of ancient mythology and Medieval theology have been banished by new astronomical discovery, and complains that "all its poetry is lost," but Lumen responds angrily to this plaint:

> "Do you not know that truth is immeasurably more beautiful, grander, and infinitely more marvellous than error, however that may be embellished? What can be comparable in all the mythologies past and present, to the rapt scientific contemplation of celestial grandeurs and the sublime movements of nature? What impression can strike the soul more profoundly than the fact of the expanse crowded with worlds, and the immensity of the sidereal systems? What voice is more eloquent than a star-lit night? What wild flight of imagination could conceive an image surpassing that of the

interstellar voyage of light, stamping with the
seal of eternity the transitory events of the life
of each world?"[6]

It is arguable, I think, that in Poe's "Mesmeric Revelation" and *Eureka*, and in Flammarion's "History of a
Comet" and *Lumen*, we have four of the purest examples of
"scientific romance"—or, if you will, celebrations of "the
Poetry of Science." They are not works of science, nor are
they didactic exercises in the popularization of science. They
are works which bring their readers into confrontation with
the implications of theories and speculations about the nature
of the universe. We must not forget that "the universe"—
whether we mean by that the grander universe of Poe's design or the mere physical universe of stars—is an hypothesis;
its image is something we construct. This process of con-
struction is no mere fitting together of data as if the data
were pieces of a jigsaw puzzle. To imagine the universe is to
make a great effort of imagination; to struggle with the scale
of cosmic distances and the idea of infinity, to grasp and
comprehend the implications of our observations with respect to the beginning and the end of our world, our solar
system, and our cosmos. We may try to do this as rationally
as we can, but even if we are Sadducees or positivists, declining to avail ourselves of such hypotheses as God or the
soul, still we cannot avoid the vault of the imagination, the
mental gyration, the creative synthesis which gives rise to
that triumphant cry of achievement: Eureka! I have found it!
To say that this is, in essence, an aesthetic achievement, is
not to say that we are being necessarily unscientific, and we
must surely agree with *Lumen*, that the joy and sense of triumph which are the most desirable are those which come
from the conviction that one has grasped the truth and put
aside an old error.

The cosmic perspective, which is what *Eureka* tries
to teach us, is indeed something which we must learn. But it
is not something which can be learned in the way that we
learn to recognize objects in our environment. It is not something that an animal could ever learn. The universe is not
something we discover in the sense that we discover the

screwdriver that we had lost, or in the sense that we discover
gold by panning for it; it is something we have to add to our
perceptions by a creative effort, and when we learn to look at
things anew we are operating as artists as well as scientists,
extrapolating a whole out of disparate parts as well as reducing a complexity to its constituent elements. The universe is
not something we see through telescopes, but something we
see all around us with our naked eyes, if we know how. "To
see a World in a Grain of Sand/ And Heaven in a Wild
Flower,/ Hold Infinity in the palm of your hand/ And Eternity in an hour" is how Blake represents it in the first verse
of "Auguries of Innocence." This, I think, is what Poe means
at the end of his romance when he says that the Heart Divine,
whose systolic sequence is the life-cycle of the universe, is
also our own heart: the sustaining motor of our life, our intelligence and our power of apprehension.

If *Eureka* is to be judged, as Poe asks us to judge it,
as a poem or a romance, then we must ask whether it is a
good poem or romance. There are several ways in which we
might look for merit within it, but I think because of the kind
of work it is we must not be content with the ordinary canons
of literary criticism, which will direct our attention to the
elegance of its prose. As a poem in prose, it is certainly not
as pretty as "Shadow" or "The Masque of the Red Death,"
and as a romance it certainly has not the dramatic tension of
"The Gold Bug" or "The Narrative of Arthur Gordon Pym."
But given its nature, we should not assess it either simply by
the canons of scientific accuracy. Despite some interesting
anticipations of later theory, it cannot commend itself as a
logical analysis of the astronomical data of its day. If we are
fairly to weigh *Eureka*, and if we are fairly to weigh those
works which echo it, from Flammarion through Wells and
Hodgson and Stapledon to the rhapsodic elements in the
work of Arthur C. Clarke, Poul Anderson, and Carl Sagan,
then we must consider the uniqueness of its aesthetic task:
the making of a version of that most fabulous and most fascinating of hypotheses, the universe. We must ask how the
aesthetics of *Eureka* compare with the aesthetics of Aristotle,
of Copernicus, of Giordano Bruno, of Swedenborg, and of
Einstein. If we do that, then I think we must conclude that it

is not a great work. It is not so very original, and not so very clear, sharp or dramatic. On the other hand, it is by no means a poor work; there is nothing shoddy about it, nothing careless—it is not hackwork, and if it is read in the right spirit it still has the power to renew the imagination of the reader in his own struggle for Enlightenment.

VI.

AN INTRODUCTION
TO ALTERNATE WORLDS

An alternate world—some writers and commentators prefer the designation "alternative world" on grammatical grounds—is an account of Earth as it might have become in consequence of some hypothetical alteration in history. Serious essays in speculative history and "mainstream" novels employing the device tend to deal with alternate histories on a singular basis, but many science fiction stories hypothesize a system of parallel worlds, sometimes called a "multiverse," as a framework in which many alternate worlds can be simultaneously held. In many SF stories these parallel alternate worlds can and do interact with one another. The "many worlds interpretation" of quantum-mechanical uncertainties has given a gloss of respectability to this notion by suggesting that there might indeed be an ever-proliferating multiverse which includes all possible alternative universes.

Hypothetical exercises of this kind have long been popular with historians. Their virtue was proclaimed by Isaac d'Israeli in one of the essays in *The Curiosities of Literature* (3 volumes, 1791-1823). The best-known anthology of such essays is *If It Had Happened Otherwise* (1931, expanded 1972; also known as *If; or, History Rewritten*), edited by J. C. Squire (hereafter referred to simply as *If*). Squire took his inspiration from G. M. Trevelyan's essay, "If Napoleon Had Won the Battle of Waterloo," which was published in the same year (1907) as Joseph Chamberlin's twenty-two-essay collection, *The Ifs of History. If*'s contribu-

tors included G. K. Chesterton, André Maurois, Hilaire Bel-
loc, A. J. P. Taylor, and Winston Churchill.

The first novels investigating alternate histories were
written in French. Louis-Napoléon Geoffroy's *Napoléon
apocryphe* (1836) offers a rousing account of Napoleon's
successful conquest of the entire world and the ensuing era
of world peace, while Charles Renouvier's *Uchronie* (1857)
alters Roman history in such a way that the decaying Roman
Empire never became Christian. The first such story in English is usually reckoned to have been Edward Everett Hale's
"Hands Off" (1881), a *conte philosophique* concerned with
the theory of determinism, but it was preceded by Nathaniel
Hawthorne's eccentric account of "P's Correspondence"
(1845), in which letters sent from London include descriptions of the alternative fates of various notable individuals,
including Byron, Shelley, Keats, and Napoleon.

The first full-length alternate history novel in English
was probably Castello N. Holford's *Aristopia* (1895), which
offers an alternative history of the U.S.A. A novel of marginal interest published in Britain shortly afterwards is *The
Phantom Army* (1898) by Max Pemberton, which describes
the exploits of a "modern Napoleon" whose campaigns take
place in the 1890s. Although the story begins five years earlier than the book's publication date it is indistinguishable in
content from many other imaginary war novels of its day and
the problem of its classification illustrates the phenomenon
by which all near-future novels dealing with large-scale
events are tacitly transformed into alternate histories by the
passage of time.

Pemberton's book might well have inspired the not-
dissimilar *Trafalgar Refought* (1905) by W. Laird Clowes
and Alan H. Burgoyne, which describes how the battle of
Trafalgar might have turned out had it been fought a hundred
years later. Military historians have been more keenly interested in alternative histories than any others because they
deal with such dramatic and clear-cut historical turning-
points; serious war gamers dedicated to the endless replaying
of classic battles, examining the consequences of various
tactical decisions, are of course engaged in the continual
generation of alternate histories.

* * * * * * *

The hard core of the alternate history genre has always concerned itself with alternative outcomes to significant wars; an early American example is F. P. Williams's *Hallie Williams* (1900), which was the first of several works speculating as to what might have happened had the Confederacy won the American Civil War. Notable later examples include Winston Churchill's ingenious double-switch essay "If Lee Had Not Won the Battle of Gettysburg" in Squire's *If*; Ward Moore's meticulous and effective novel *Bring the Jubilee* (1953); and MacKinlay Kantor's essay, "If the South Had Won the Civil War" (1960; expanded into book form, 1961). Other early examples of exercises in alternate military history include Maurice Baring's "The Alternative" (1922), which features an alternative Napoleon humbler by far than Geoffroy's, and Arthur Conan Doyle's "The Death Voyage" (1929), which features an alternative climax to World War I.

Luridly alarmist futuristic novels had become very popular in Britain in the decades before World War I and novels describing its possible outcome continued to appear in profusion once the oft-anticipated conflict actually got under way. H. H. Munro's description of life in conquered England, *When William Came* (1914), was not an alternate history novel when it first appeared, but it had become one by the time it was reprinted in the 1920s. It provided a template for many novels written during and after World War II—which inevitably became the principal focus of interest for alternate historians after 1945 and remains so to this day.

Novels in which Hitler and his allies are victorious in World War II written while that was still a real possibility include *Loss of Eden* (1940, also known as *If Hitler Comes* 1941) by Douglas Brown and Christopher Serpell, *When the Bells Rang* (1943) by Anthony Armstrong and Bruce Graeme, and *When Adolf Came* (1943) by Martin Hawkin. The many authentic exercises in alternate history dealing with the same theme include Sarban's *The Sound of His Horn* (1952), Cyril M. Kornbluth's "Two Dooms" (1958), C. S. Forester's essay "If Hitler Had Invaded England" (1960),

William L. Shirer's essay "If Hitler Had Won World War II" (1961), Philip K. Dick's *The Man in the High Castle* (1962), the film *It Happened Here* (1963), Hilary Bailey's "The Fall of Frenchy Steiner" (1964), Norman Longmate's *If Britain Had Fallen* (1972), Keith Roberts's "Weihnachtsabend" (1972), Frederick Mullally's *Hitler Has Won* (1975), Len Deighton's *SS-GB* (1978), Philip Mackie's television serial *An Englishman's Castle* (1978), William Overgard's *The Divide* (1980), Brad Linaweaver's *Moon of Ice* (short version 1982, expanded 1988), James P. Hogan's *The Proteus Operation* (1985), and Robert Harris's *Fatherland* (1992). An anthology of eleven such stories is *Hitler Victorious* (1986) edited by Gregory Benford and Martin H. Greenberg.

Most stories of Hitler victorious are, of course, horror stories; it is relatively rare for anyone to put in a good word for a successful Third Reich, although David Dvorkin's *Budspy* (1987) is relatively even-handed in its contemplation of a world in which peace was achieved without Nazi Germany's demolition. Other notable alternate histories involving World War II include *The Burning Mountain* (1983) by Alfred Coppel, which describes the invasion of Japan after the failure of the Manhattan project; "The Lucky Strike" (1984) by Kim Stanley Robinson, in which a US pilot refuses to drop the atom bomb on Hiroshima; and *Elleander Morning* (1985) by Jerry Yulsman, which describes a world where Hitler was assassinated before he could start the war. Because World War II is the more recent, its alternate histories have inevitably crowded out modern works featuring alternative versions of World War I, which are relatively few in number; however, one notable recent addition to their tally is Guido Morselli's *Past Conditional* (1975, translated into English 1981).

* * * * * * *

The idea of alternate worlds was introduced to genre science fiction in appropriately spectacular fashion by Murray Leinster in "Sidewise in Time" (1934), in which timeslips turn the earth's surface into a patchwork of alternate histories. Most of the SF stories which subsequently developed the notion were similarly profligate in their whole-sale deployment of implicitly-infinite sets of alternate worlds.

Stanley Weinbaum's "The Worlds of If" (1935) is a light comedy, but it was inevitable that the melodramatic potential inherent in the idea should come quickly to the fore. Alternate worlds first went to war in Jack Williamson's *The Legion of Time* (1938; in book form 1952), in which the incipiently paradoxical conflict—whose ultimate prize is, of course, actuality—ranges across vast expanses of time. The idea of worlds battling for existence by attempting to maintain the coherency of their own history was further developed by Fritz Leiber, first in *Destiny Times Three* (1945), and subsequently in the "Change War" series, which includes the fine short novel *The Big Time* (1958, in book form 1961). Attempts by "potential futures" to influence the present by means of friendlier persuasion were presented by C. L. Moore in "Greater than Gods" (1939) and by Ross Rocklynne in "The Diversifal" (1951).

The science-fictional notion of competing alternative histories was quickly recomplicated by SF writers in stories of time travel in which the heroes range across a vast series of parallel worlds, each featuring a different alternative history. The policing of time-tracks—either singly, as in Isaac Asimov's *The End of Eternity* (1955), which features the totalitarian control of history by social engineers, or in great profusion—became a popular theme in SF during the 1950s. The exploits of such police forces are featured in Sam Merwin's *House of Many Worlds* (1951) and *Three Faces of Time* (1955), H. Beam Piper's "Paratime" series, begun with "Time Crime" (1955), Poul Anderson's "Time Patrol" series, whose early stories are collected in *Guardians of Time* (1960), and John Brunner's *Times Without Number* (1962). Simon Hawke's "Time Wars" series, begun with *The Ivanhoe Gambit* (1984) and continued in many sequels, uses the notion to comic as well as melodramatic effect.

More extravagant conflicts across and between time-lines are displayed in Keith Laumer's *Worlds of the Imperium* (1962) and its sequels, Avram Davidson's *Masters of the Maze* (1965), Jack Chalker's *Downtiming the Night Side*

(1985), Frederik Pohl's *The Coming of the Quantum Cats* (1986), Mike McQuay's *Memories* (1987), and Michael P. Kube-McDowell's *Alternities* (1988). The most grandiose attempt to establish totalitarian control of time is featured in *The Fall of Chronopolis* (1974) by Barrington J. Bayley. Not all works of this kind are lightweight adventure stories; John Crowley's excellent "Great Work of Time" (1989) is a deeply thoughtful work about a conspiracy of well-intentioned imperialists whose attempts to use time-machines to take charge of history never quite produce the desired result.

* * * * * * *

The first careful attempt to construct a plausible alternative history in SF was L. Sprague de Camp's *Lest Darkness Fall* (1939, in book form 1941), in which a man slips back through time and sets out to remould history by attempting to prevent—or at least ameliorate—the advent of the Dark Ages. In attempting to extrapolate his plot in a scrupulously logical manner, de Camp engaged basic questions of historical determinism, coming (inevitably) to the conclusion that the most important agents of historical change are not battles but relatively humble technological innovations whose consequences often pass unnoticed by contemporary commentators. De Camp later took care, however, to point out the limitations of technological determinism in the wry parable of "Aristotle and the Gun" (1958). In the more orthodox but less earnest "The Wheels of If" (1940), de Camp displayed a contemporary America which might have resulted from tenth-century colonization by Norsemen.

Most subsequent SF stories in the earnestly extrapolative vein tend to avoid any elaborate description of historical developments and any meticulous analysis of historical causation, but SF writers with a keen interest in history do sometimes devote considerable care to the development of imaginary pasts. Robert Silverberg's several adventures in alternate history are invariably well-researched and cleverly worked-out. The alternate history used in his fine "young adult" novel *The Gate of Worlds* (1967) is further explored by Silverberg, John Brunner, and Chelsea Quinn Yarbro in the interesting "shared world anthology" *Beyond the Gate of Worlds* (1991). The historical background to S. M. Stirling's "Draka" series begun with *Marching Through Georgia* (1988) is also worked out in some detail, the explanations being relegated to appendices to the melodramatic texts.

One of the most effective images of an alternate history produced within the SF genre is contained in Keith Roberts's story-series *Pavane* (1968), which describes a technologically-primitive scenario generated by the failure of the Reformation and the subsequent Industrial Revolution. This echoes Max Weber's sociological thesis proposing that the spread of the "protestant ethic" was a vital precursor of capitalist enterprise, and hence of the Industrial Revolution. Outside of crucial military victories, the failure of the Reformation is the most common historical pivot evoked by alternate historians within and without the SF genre, although it is sometimes transposed into military terms by making the success of the Spanish Armada a key event. The existence of a theory which can be used to justify the patterns of extrapolation within stories is one thing which attracts writers to this kind of scenario; another is the fact that it is somewhat easier for a writer to deal with alternative presents in which technological progress has been slowed down—so that they more-or-less resemble the actual past—than with scenarios in which it is accelerated. Accelerated progress stories are not unknown, though; notable examples include D. R. Bensen's *And Having Writ....* (1978) and James White's *The Silent Stars Go By* (1991), the latter featuring an alternate history in which the first interstellar spacecraft is launched in 1491.

Tampering with such events as the Reformation provides an opportunity for writers to examine the general role of religions in history. Bolder exercises in this vein were uncommon in the early part of the century, for reasons of diplomacy, but have inevitably attracted more attention in recent years. John Boyd's *The Last Starship from Earth* (1969) was the first novel to investigate what might have happened had the crucifixion never taken place. Harry Turtledove's

81

series whose early stories are collected in *Agent of Byzantium* (1987) is set in a world in which Mohammed became a Christian and Islam never became a competitive ideological force. Other writers, as might be expected, have taken an interest in scenarios in which Christianity was less historically successful. L. Neil Smith's *The Crystal Empire* (1986) describes a world in which Christendom was destroyed in the fourteenth century while Islam thrived. Kim Newman and Eugene Byrne's "The Wandering Christian" (1991) ironically depicts a world in which the immortal Wandering Jew is the only man left in Medieval Europe who remembers that there ever were such persons as Jesus and his disciples.

* * * * * * *

In recent times alternate history stories have become extremely fashionable in genre SF, becoming a popular framework for theme anthologies, each of which—by necessity—presents a spectrum of alternatives and thus tends tacitly to reinforce the notion that our own universe is indeed only one strand in an incredibly complex multiversal weave. The series of What Might Have Been anthologies edited by Gregory Benford and Martin H. Greenberg—which followed up the success of their earlier *Hitler Victorious*—currently extends to four volumes: *Alternate Empires* (1989), *Alternate Heroes* (1990), *Alternate Wars* (1991), and *Alternate Americas* (1992), while Mike Resnick is continuing another series which so far includes *Alternate Kennedys* (1992), *Alternate Presidents* (1992), and *Alternate Warriors* (1993). Individual works which similarly promote the notion of a bewildering confusion of alternate histories include John M. Ford's series begun with "Mandalay" (1979), and Michael Flynn's "The Forest of Time" (1987), both of which confront lost time-travellers with the near-impossibly of their ever getting home again.

The reasons for this dramatic upsurge in the popularity of alternate world stories are complicated, but several patterns of preoccupation can be identified in the fiction itself. The phenomenon is connected with the several ways in which Americans have been forced to re-evaluate their own

BRIAN STABLEFORD

history and the processes of mythologization which turned that history into a triumphant progress of freedom, democracy and all-conquering frontiersmanship. The fact that the voices of native Americans and black Americans, so long abandoned to cry in the wilderness, have at last made themselves heard, has prompted some guilt-stricken reappraisal and subsequent lamentation of the fates of the native populations of the Americas and the slaves transported to labor in the various colonies. This newly-hatched sense of doubt has expanded to take in even the most taken-for-granted aspects of American culture, including its stern opposition to socialist movements.

Science fiction has provided a useful medium for the expression of such lamentations and alternate histories have provided a useful vehicle for such reappraisals. Alternate histories of America which attempt to deal with sensitive political issues of this kind are frequently to the fore in the anthologies listed above; novel-length exercises in a similar vein include Gordon Eklund's *All Times Possible* (1974), Orson Scott Card's fantasy series begun with *Seventh Son* (1987), and Terry Bisson's *Fire on the Mountain* (1988). L. Neil Smith's *The Probability Broach* (1980) and its sequels, by contrast, imagine an America whose history resulted in an even braver incarnation of the Libertarian dream. Views of American history from beyond its shores tend, understandably, to be somewhat less reverent; the series of stories by Kim Newman and Eugene Byrne begun with "In the Air" (1990), set in a communist America ruled by Al Capone, provides a striking example.

The complicity of science fiction in the ideological sins of modern America has not escaped examination in this way. It is subjected to scathing criticism in Norman Spinrad's ingenious *The Iron Dream* (1972), which reproduces the text of a "classic" novel in which the immigrant pulp SF writer named Adolf Hitler sublimated all the paranoid anxieties and dreams of conquest which, in some other world, might have made him a dangerous man.

* * * * * * *

By comparison with the alternate histories of science fiction, the alternate histories of "mainstream" fiction seem distinctly staid, distorting history in fairly minimal ways and exploring relatively modest consequences of its alteration. Alternative outcomes of World War II have long dominated the mainstream alternate history novel, but there are sufficient examples of other kinds to support the notion of a more general mainstream "tradition" of alternate history running in parallel to the much more prolific genre SF tradition. The device is sometimes used satirically, as in R. Egerton Swartout's *It Might Have Happened* (1934), Marghanita Laski's *Tory Heaven* (1948), and Kingsley Amis's *The Alteration* (1976) or comically, as in Jack Finney's *The Woodrow Wilson Dime* (1968), but more earnest treatments predominate. Notable examples of earnest mainstream alternate history include Oscar Lewis's *The Lost Years* (1951), John Hersey's *White Lotus* (1965), Vladimir Nabokov's *Ada* (1969), Martin Cruz Smith's *The Indians Won* (1970), Douglas Jones's *The Court Martial of George Armstrong Custer* (1976), and Martin Green's *The Earth Again Redeemed* (1978). An interesting pair of mainstream novels is Ronald W. Clark's *Queen Victoria's Bomb* (1967) and *The Bomb That Failed* (1969, also known as *The Last Year of the Old World*), in the first of which the atom bomb is developed in Victorian times, while in the second its appearance on the historical scene is delayed.

Regrettably, there are relatively few twentieth-century *contes philosophiques* in English which attempt to follow Edward Everett Hale's precedent in addressing the philosophical implications of the notion of alternate histories. It is rather ironic that there is more philosophical discourse to be found in wild sciencefictional melodramas like Bayley's *Fall of Chronopolis* than there is in the far more sober and ostensibly more contemplative treatments of mainstream writers. J. B. Priestley's fascination with time encouraged him to touch on the theme, but only barely, in *Dangerous Corner* (1932) and other plays. The literary traditions of other languages have, however, always been more hospitable to *contes philosophiques*, and it is not surprising that alternate worlds crop up in the work of Jorge Luis Bor-

ges's—most notably in the surreal "Tlön, Uqbar, Orbis Ter-
tius" (in *Ficciones*, 1944, translated 1962)—and his sometime collaborator Adolfo Bioy Casares's—notably the enigmatic "The Celestial Plot" (in *La trama celeste*, 1948, translated in *The Invention of Morel and Other Stories*, 1964).

In recent years the many worlds interpretation of un-
certainty has encouraged a good deal of philosophical discourse in non-fiction, but few writers have used fiction to
explore the existential implications of the notion. Such ex-
ceptions as there are have usually fallen into the SF genre for
want of any other marketing strategy, although they fit rather
uneasily into it; these include Brian W. Aldiss's parallel
worlds story *Report on Probability A* (1968), Michel Jeury's
Chronolysis (1973 as *Le Temps incertain*, translated 1980),
Robert Anton Wilson's Schrödinger's Cat trilogy (1979-81),
and Graham Dunstan Martin's *Time-Slip* (1986).

* * * * * * *

A notable early meditation on some of the philosophical implications of alternativity is Guy Dent's *Emperor of
the If* (1926), which was also the first work to broaden out
the theme to take in alternate prehistories, its opening section
imagining the world as it might have become had the earth's
climate not cooled during the Ice Ages, and the "men" who
might have evolved instead of us. Other notable exercises in
alternative evolution include Harry Harrison's series *West of
Eden* (1984), in which the dinosaurs never became extinct;
the stories collected in Harry Turtledove's *A Different Flesh*
(1988), in which the first Europeans to reach the New World
find it inhabited by half-human "Sims"; and two stories of
my own: *The Empire of Fear* (1989), in which an alien infection permits a kind of "vampirism" to flourish in Europe following Attila's invasion; and "Complications" (1992), in
which all vertebrate species—including humans—have
males which live parasitically inside the bodies of females.

Alternative universes whose physical make-up is different at the most basic level were first described in nineteenth-century accounts of two-dimensional worlds, and they
are featured wholesale in George Gamow's series of educa-

tive parables *Mr. Tompkins in Wonderland* (1939), but this kind of imaginative extravagance was not accommodated in alternate world stories until fairly recently. Stories imagining alternate cosmologies include Barrington J. Bayley's "Me and My Antronoscope" (1973) and Ted Chiang's "Tower of Babylon" (1990), while the alternate physical chemistry of phlogiston theory is extrapolated to apocalyptic effect in Howard Waldrop's "...the World, as We Know't" (1982). A multiverse of universes with different physical laws is partially explored in Frederik Pohl and Jack Williamson's *The Singers of Time* (1990).

The dearth of philosophically-inclined uses of the alternate worlds theme outside the SF ghetto was eventually compensated by the work of genre writer Philip K. Dick, whose work may yet become as influential outside the genre as it has been within it. Dick's use of the theme usually involves the world-views of individual characters rather than objectively-defined diverted histories, and the essential intimacy of his approach frequently allows him to develop a remarkable narrative intensity. His classic alternate world story remains the Axis-victorious novel *The Man in the High Castle*, but this also needs to be studied in the context of such distorted-perception stories as *Eye in the Sky* (1957), *Now Wait for Last Year* (1967), and *Flow My Tears, the Policeman Said* (1974). Intriguing homage is paid to Dick's distinctive use of the theme by Michael Bishop's *The Secret Ascension* (1987, also known as *Philip K. Dick Is Dead, Alas*), which describes an alternate present in which Dick became famous for his non-SF works (which only achieved posthumous publication in our world) but was later suppressed as a dissident, his SF circulating covertly in samizdat form. Some of the highly idiosyncratic works of R. A. Lafferty also involve the surreal deployment of alternate worlds, most notably the short novel "The Three Armageddons of Enniscorthy Sweeney" in *Apocalypses* (1977).

Other novels which use alternate worlds to explore more intimate questions of alternativity, often bringing the philosophical problem of identity into focus, include Bob Shaw's *The Two-Timers* (1968), Joanna Russ's *The Female Man* (1975), Sheila Finch's *Infinity's Web* (1985), Josephine

Saxton's *Queen of the States* (1986) Ken Grimwood's *Replay* (1986), and Thomas Berger's *Changing the Past* (1989). The three novels on this list by female writers all use alternative versions of the central character cleverly to confront and explore the existential and psychological problems associated with living as a female in a male-dominated world.

* * * * * * *

In recent years the alternate history sub-genre has been enriched and enlivened by the contributions of a curious overlapping sub-genre which generally goes by the name "steampunk" (coined, of course, by mocking analogy with "cyberpunk"). Steampunk stories are generally set in an alternative nineteenth century—very often in Britain, although almost all the authors involved are American—which is based as much in literary images as in actual history, often mingling actual historical persons and fictitious characters.

Pioneering steampunk stories included Stephen Utley and Howard Waldrop's "Black as the Pit, from Pole to Pole" (1977) and K. W. Jeter's *Morlock Night* (1979), but it is possible retrospectively to identify a number of "proto-steampunk" stories, notably including Harry Harrison's *Tunnel Through the Deeps* (1972, also known as *A Transatlantic Tunnel, Hurrah!*) and Poul Anderson's *A Midsummer Tempest* (1974), and it is arguable that the deepest roots of the sub-genre are to be found in Michael Moorcock's "Nomad of Time" trilogy, begun with *The Warlord of the Air* (1971). Neither of the first two stories named are alternate histories in the strictest sense, but Harrison's and Anderson's novels are, and Moorcock's trilogy partakes of the gaudy multiversal background common to the vast majority of his extraordinarily varied works. Many works which followed in the footsteps of the pioneers of steampunk are straightforward alternate histories; others highlight certain awkward problems in trying to set the boundaries of the alternate history sub-genre.

Utley and Waldrop had earlier collaborated on "Custer's Last Jump" (1976), a cleverly-framed story set in an alternate history in which aeroplanes and other advanced machinery have made little enough difference to the Civil War; Waldrop went on to write other tales in the same ironic and eccentric vein, including "Fin de Cycle" (1990) and "The Night of the Cooters," (1987) the latter being one of a rapidly-expanding set of stories which take place in the world of H. G. Wells's *The War of the Worlds*, treated as if it were an alternative history. Although the tendency to borrow bits of past writers' imagined presents and near-futures—often in eccentric combination, treating them as if they were alternate histories—is not confined to steampunk stories, many steampunk stories use the device in very striking fashion. Modern tales of Sherlock Holmes have now become so numerous, and so promiscuous in matching him against other literary characters (Mr. Hyde, Dracula, Fu Manchu, Wells's Martians) and "real-world" persons (Jack the Ripper, Freud, Wilfred Rhodes) that Holmesian London might easily be deemed to have become an alternate world—or a series of alternate worlds—in its own right.

The most outstanding steampunk alternate world stories are Rudy Rucker's *The Hollow Earth* (1990), which features an alternate Edgar Allan Poe who knows only too well whereof he writes; William Gibson and Bruce Sterling's *The Difference Engine* (1990), in which Babbage's calculating machine precipitates an information-technology revolution in Victorian England; and Kim Newman's *Anno Dracula* (1992), which is a bizarre "sequel" to an alternative version of Bram Stoker's *Dracula*, in which the count thwarts his enemies and marries Queen Victoria. Only the second of these three refuses to include borrowed fictional characters alongside its actual ones.

Some steampunk novels accommodate magic just as readily—and as comfortably—as they accommodate such science-fictional devices as time travel. Tim Powers's *The Anubis Gates* (1985) and *The Stress of Her Regard* (1989) take too few liberties with known history to be considered true alternate world stories, but Esther Friesner's *Druid's Blood* (1988) is much more cavalier in setting Dr. Watson and a substitute Sherlock Holmes loose in a dramatically-transfigured (and blithely anachronistic) Victorian London where magic works on a grand scale. The practice of constructing worlds which are historically very similar to ours, save for the single modification that the magic in which their inhabitants believe is actually workable, is also much more widespread than the steampunk sub-genre, and also raises an awkward question as to whether such stories can be considered to be exercises in alternative history. The "science fiction" and "alternate world" labels have long been applied to one such set of stories—Randall Garrett's "Lord D'Arcy" series, which comprises the novel *Too Many Magicians* (1967) and two collections—but there may be grounds for taking aboard a good many other intensively-researched "hard fantasy" stories (Orson Scott Card's "Alvin Maker" series has already been cited above).

* * * * * * *

The "anything goes" spirit of steampunk may seem to be a far cry from disciplined attempts to imagine how history might have worked out differently had some crucial event happened otherwise, but it is worth noting that its characteristic tone is not so very far removed from the flamboyantly sarcastic temper of many of the essays in Squire's *If*. There is something about the notion of alternate history which brings out a fondness for bizarrerie even in serious historians. When they begin to extrapolate they are very often inclined to desert the highway of maximum plausibility for the byways of irony, and are easily led to take great delight in the kind of imaginative snowball effect by which apparently-trivial events become magnified into the fall of empires ("For want of a nail, the shoe was lost..." etc, etc).

The study of history, however scientifically it may be approached, does have an inherent aesthetic component—as, of course, all sciences do. The aesthetics of history are intimately bound up with the awesome intricacy of patterns of cause and effect, which are so frequently hidden from the consciousness of the actors involved. The aesthetics of history make the exploration of alternative histories very tempting—too tempting for quibbles about the impossibility of finding safe answers to "counterfactual questions" to prohibit their production. It must be remembered, too, that it is when imaginative exercises in alternate history are at their most extravagantly whimsical that they tend to touch on—and thus to illuminate and dramatize—deeper questions of determinism, utilitarian ethics, and so on. There is no conflict, in *contes philosphiques*, between playfulness and seriousness; the two can and ought to work hand-in-hand.

Until now, alternate world stories have been the province of recently small groups of *cognoscenti*. They have remained relatively opaque to general readers uneducated in the ways of historians and science fiction writers, but this situation is changing as the literary strategy becomes more familiar. It will soon be the case that such stories are acceptable in all arenas of popular culture, because all potential readers and viewers will have the capacity to recognize, understand and enjoy them. The scope for such stories is infinite and in spite of a recent explosion of activity the surface has barely been scratched. The past may be dead, but all the pasts that might have been are wide open to imaginative exploration.

I can think of no better way to end this essay than to echo—more sceptically than he—a supposition advanced by J. C. Squire in the introduction to his classic volume of essays. "Few [historians]," he observes, "would pause and sadly think, when presented with the conjecture 'If Sodom and Gomorrah had not been Destroyed', how much brighter the subsequent human story would have been had the calamity been averted."[1]

Well, maybe not, but one can't help but wonder....

AFTERWORD: A NOTE ON THE TERMINOLOGY

Some years ago I used the term "alternate world" in front of Brian Aldiss, who took me to task for it. "They should be called alternative worlds," he said. "Calling them alternate worlds makes it sound as if they somehow take turns."

I took this criticism to heart because there is a sense in which, being the author of the relevant article in Peter Nicholls's definitive *Encyclopedia of Science Fiction* (1979),

I might be held to be "in charge" of this particular item of science-fictional terminology. Stricken by guilt, I decided to do the only thing an honorable SF writer could do—I wrote a story in which the alternate worlds really did take turns. I called it "Alternate Worlds" and sent it off to *Interzone*, whose editor bought it but insisted on changing the title to "Minimoments" (1990). Such is life.

When the time eventually came for me to revise the relevant article for the new (1993) edition of the encyclopedia edited by John Clute and Peter Nicholls, I thought long and hard about altering it. In the end—torn between striking a blow for justified pedantry and annoying the technical editor (who would have had to alter hundreds of cross-references)—I left the designation as it was, but added the same rider that appears in the first sentence of this article.

I admit that this is not a satisfactory solution, but common usage has now established the term "alternate worlds" so securely that it is probably beyond anyone's power to change it. The unsympathetic reviewer of Newt Gingrich and William R. Fortschen's *1945* (1995) who recently suggested that the subgenre ought to be called "suppository fiction" is, mercifully, unlikely to get his way.

VII.

ADOLF HITLER:
HIS PART IN OUR STRUGGLE

(A BRIEF ECONOMIC HISTORY
OF BRITISH SF MAGAZINES)

As *Interzone* reaches its tenth anniversary, it has already become the fourth most prolific British SF magazine, having published more issues than *Nebula* (41), but not yet as many as *Authentic* (85), *Science Fantasy/Impulse* (81 + 12), or the oft-reincarnated *New Worlds* (more than 200). It is appropriate that we should celebrate its birthday by looking back at the history of its predecessors, so that its readers may better understand its position in that Great Chain of Being which is British SF.

As most of its readers will know, *Interzone* began life a gleam in the eye of an eight-man collective, whose motives in launching it were uncommercial. They were members of a quasi-masonic inner circle of the British SF community, who shared a deep conviction that there really ought to be a British SF magazine, to celebrate the Britishness of British SF and to function as a forcing-ground for new domestic talent. In this they were carrying forward a tradition; almost all the British SF magazines which have existed were born of similar uncommercial enthusiasms. In view of this fact, it may seem eccentric to present an economic history of British SF magazines rather than a critical one, but if we are to understand the strange and rather sad history of these entities we can only do so if we see them in their true light: as starry-eyed ventures launched into a cruel and unpredictable world where the laws of supply and demand have worked in an exceptionally wayward fashion.

I have before me as I write a battered copy of the first-ever issue of *New Worlds*—not the one which Ted Carnell and Frank Arnold persuaded Stephen Frances (alias Hank Janson) to launch under the Pendulum Publications imprint in 1946, but the March 1939 issue, the first of what turned out to be a run of four produced by means of a primitive duplicator. It contains a story by John Victor Peterson, a British writer who had already made five appearances in the American SF pulps, and a discussion of his writing methods by one "Thornton Ayre." Ayre was actually the same person as the "John Cotton" whose story in the inaugural issue of *Science Fiction* is so highly praised in the news column of the same issue: John Russell Fearn. Fearn was by far and away the most prolific of the half-dozen or so British writers who had sold material to the American SF magazines, and both Ayre and Fearn were to be listed on the contents page of the first issue of the "professional" *New Worlds*.

The swift demise of this frail and fragile version of *New Worlds* was caused by the same event that caused the demise of many other periodicals: the outbreak of the Second World War. Had it not been for Adolf Hitler, and the disruption of the economic affairs of Britain which resulted—directly and indirectly—from his activities, the history of British SF magazines might have been very different. It was Hitler's war which spoiled all the early attempts to launch British SF magazines, and it was the artificial economic situation which existed after that war's end which determined the nature and the fortunes of the second generation of such magazines.

* * * * * * *

The story of British SF magazines might be said to have begun with an experimental weekly boys' paper called *Scoops*, published by the firm founded by C. Arthur Pearson, whose turn-of-the-century magazines had done so much to promote scientific romance by publishing important early work by George Griffith, H. G. Wells, and M. P. Shiel. But *Scoops* lasted only twenty issues in the Spring of 1934, and did not use the term "science fiction," which had not yet been imported from the US pulp magazines as a generic label. It serialized Professor A. M. Low's "Space" (reprinted as *Adrift in the Stratosphere*), reprinted Conan Doyle's *The Poison Belt*, and—inevitably—featured some early work by John Russell Fearn, but it was not aimed at an adult audience and its brief existence is merely a curiosity to be noted.

The real history of British SF begins with the growth of a community of fans who had discovered SF in imported American SF pulps. They were moved to communicate with one another and to organize themselves by the founding of the Science Fiction League in Hugo Gernsback's *Wonder Stories*—a cunning marketing device which gave birth to the strange world of SF fandom. There were five British chapters of the SFL, and it was under the aegis of one of them— the Nuneaton branch—that Maurice Hanson began issuing in 1936 the forerunner of *New Worlds*, a fanzine called *Novae Terrae*.

Novae Terrae was soon joined—and overtaken—by a more regular and much more handsome periodical: *Scientifiction: The British Fantasy Review*. *Scientifiction* was edited by journalist Walter Gillings, whose professional contacts enabled him to have it printed in a proper manner, rather than being run off on a duplicator. Its first issue (February 1937) included an interview with John Beynon Harris, at that time the second most successful British writer of pulp SF, and hopeful articles about the future of British SF by three of the others: Benson Herbert, Festus Pragnell, and John Russell Fearn. It also carried news of the first ever "conference of British fantasy fans," which was organized in Leeds by the British chapters of the Science Fiction League—a meeting which led to the founding of the (British) Science Fiction Association.

The third issue of *Scientifiction* (June 1937) was able to announce—alongside an article by Eric Frank Russell and an interview with Olaf Stapledon—the founding of Britain's very own SF pulp magazine, *Tales of Wonder and Super-Science*, also to be edited by Gillings. The announcement boasted that the first issue would include stories by all the leading British contributors to the American SF pulps; the contents page featured Benson Herbert, Festus Pragnell, Eric Frank Russell, John Beynon [Harris], and (under two different names) John Russell Fearn. *Tales of Wonder*, as it became, might well have become an established magazine; but the advent of the war killed off any hope of that. After publishing sixteen issues it fell victim to paper-rationing and to the slightly-belated conscription of its editor (who had initially been exempted as a conscientious objector).

By the time it died, *Tales of Wonder* was no longer Britain's only SF magazine. The popularity of the US pulp magazines which were sold cheaply under the label "Yank Mags" in Woolworth's had not gone unnoticed by British entrepreneurs. Some British publishers began reprinting American pulps—including a few SF titles—and others experimented with their own domestic products. The effect of the war was to cut abruptly short almost all of these experiments. Only one SF magazine—the reprint *Astounding* founded in 1939—kept going through the war years, and its size and schedule were both severely restricted by paper rationing. A second domestic SF pulp, *Fantasy*, was founded by Newnes in 1938, but it only lasted three issues before its editor was conscripted and the threat of impending paper-rationing persuaded the publisher to abort the whole venture. Its contributors included John Beynon [Harris], Eric Frank Russell, and (of course) John Russell Fearn.

Had the war not strangled British pulp magazines more-or-less at birth, an interesting competition would surely have developed between the reprinted and domestic titles. As things were, various small publishers like Gerald G. Swan and Benson Herbert's Utopian Publications continued to issue SF in an assortment of formats—usually, by necessity, very cramped—using any odd bits of paper they could lay their hands on (most of it entirely unsuitable for the purpose).

Paper rationing continued for some time after 1945, and it played a major part in shaping the subsequent patterns of British publishing. Its slow relaxation created a temporary vacuum of demand for reading-matter. Paperback books, which had never become firmly established in pre-war Britain, enjoyed a great advantage while paper was still on ration (an advantage reflected in the generous wartime allowance which had given Penguin an all-important early boost), and dozens of paperback companies sprang up, eager to exploit the window of economic opportunity. Many of these publishers copied the strategies of the American paperback companies, whose marketing methods were heavily influenced by those of the pulp magazines they replaced: books were sorted into distinct genre lines, and dressed with sensational and suggestive covers. The new British paperback publishers—eager to appeal to the lowbrow market disdained by the rather austere Penguins—did likewise.

The biggest profits made by the new British paperback companies came from hard-boiled stories of American gangsterism—including the Hank Janson books, which cashed in on the huge success of James Hadley Chase's *No Orchids for Miss Blandish*—and from slightly risqué romances of the kind mass-produced by "Paul Renin" (Richard Goyne). Inevitably, though, they began to publish science fiction too, helping to establish a market space into which British SF magazines might comfortably fit. Hamilton & Co launched the pulp-format *Futuristic Stories* and *Strange Adventures* in 1946, filling the pages with juvenile fiction by the prolific hack N. Wesley Firth, but these failed to sell and were quickly aborted. The pulp-sized Pendulum *New Worlds* initially fared no better; it suffered acute distribution difficulties, and Pendulum went bankrupt, but Ted Carnell and other regular attenders of the first-Thursday-of-every-month meetings of the London SF community (then held at the White Horse in Fetter Lane) promptly formed a new company—Nova Publications—to take it over.

In the meantime, Walter Gillings had also taken up more-or-less exactly where he had been forced to leave off by conscription. He launched a new digest-sized *Fantasy*, which featured several early stories by Arthur C. Clarke as well as the everpresent Fearn. It looked far more professional than either *Futuristic Stories* or the Pendulum *New Worlds*, and was printed on better-quality paper, but it foundered under the burden of bad distribution and rationing after publishing its third issue in 1947. Gillings reverted to fanzine publication, again using his journalistic resources to obtain professional printing for what was first called *Fantasy Review* and later *Science Fantasy Review*. In 1950 Nova Publications undertook to take responsibility for this magazine too, converting it into a fiction magazine and contracting its name to *Science-Fantasy*. This unification of the SF community was quickly spoiled by dissent; the company was too small to support two editors. As paper-rationing was gradually phased out so, alas, was Gillings; he remained a fan until he died but never lent his considerable expertise to another SF magazine until 1969-1970, when Philip Harbottle's *Vision of Tomorrow* serialized his history of British fandom, "The Impatient Dreamers." *New Worlds* and *Science-Fantasy* both came under the control of Ted Carnell, who continued to edit them until 1964.

Although several other publishers began reprinting American SF magazines, confronting the Nova magazines with stiff competition, those which retained the pulp format foundered along with their American originals. Only those which were or became digests—most notably *Astounding*, *Galaxy*, and (somewhat unsteadily) *The Magazine of Fantasy & Science Fiction*—outlasted the fifties.

* * * * * * *

In view of the earlier history of British SF one of the most surprising features of the Nova magazines was the complete absence, after the second issue of each, of John Russell Fearn. The indefatigable Fearn had found a new outlet, writing for the paperback market—which underwent explosive expansion as the restraints which had held it in check were relaxed. He produced dozens of SF novels, most of them written for Scion as "Vargo Statten" and—later—"Volsted Gridban." These bizarre names arose because paperback publishers believed in fitting authors' names to the kind of fiction they were producing; thus, gangster stories had American tough-guy names attached and risqué romances bore French-sounding pseudonyms. For his own ill-fated pioneering line of SF novels Steve Frances devised the supposedly-appropriate house pseudonym "Astron del Martia"; his competitors, perhaps unfortunately, in view of the effect it had on the public image of SF, followed his absurd lead.

The new paperback publishers paid extremely low word rates; they could get away with it, because paper-rationing had left writers as hungry as readers. Nevertheless, they were a market of sorts, and for would-be professional SF writers like Fearn, Ted Tubb (the original Volsted Gridban), and Ken Bulmer they represented a window of opportunity. It was at this point in time that the tiny community of British pulp SF writers splintered. John Beynon Harris became John Wyndham and went on to respectability. Eric Frank Russell also steered clear of the new marketplace. Some of those who dabbled in the UK paperback puddle, like Tubb and Bulmer, were soon able to graduate to the bigger and more lucrative pond that was Donald A. Wollheim's Ace Double line. Others—including Fearn—got so completely stuck in the rut of fast, mechanical production that they never got out; they went down with the cheapjack paperback companies, which shrivelled and died one by one in the fierce competition which followed the end of paper rationing. (Although John Spencer Ltd., which published four ultra-cheap and utterly dire SF magazines in the early fifties before founding the infamous Badger Books, were kept afloat for an extra ten years by the extraordinary generosity—some might call it foolishness—of the amazing Lionel Fanthorpe. Fanthorpe persisted in mass-producing books for Badger at £22 10s a time long after everybody else had either given up or started demanding more money; his 180+ volumes included most of the 108 issues of *Supernatural Stories*).

One survivor of the post-war boom-and-bust was Hamilton & Co., parent firm of Panther Books. Like Scion and Curtis Warren (whose prolific SF output was mostly supplied by one Dennis Hughes under a dozen unlikely aliases), Hamilton went in for SF on a considerable scale. After killing *Futuristic Stories* and *Strange Adventure* they began an imitation of Fearn's Vargo Statten series, optimistically naming it the "Authentic Science Fiction Series." These appeared under slightly more dignified pseudonyms—Lee Stanton, Jon J. Deegan, Roy Sheldon, etc.—than those used by their competitors, and some Hamilton authors, including Ken Bulmer and Bryan Berry, were actually allowed to use their own names on books which were given a slightly more upmarket image. The Authentic series was gradually transformed into a magazine by its editor Gordon Landsborough and the "technical editor," H. J. "Bert" Campbell, who was hired in order to give it a gloss of respectability.

Bert Campbell really was an authentic scientist—a career which he resumed in due course, publishing an excellent early book on *The Pleasure Areas*, the fascinating regions of rats' brains first discovered by James Olds—but his expertise did not add much quality to his own SF, or that of most of the authors he published while he was in sole charge of *Authentic* from 1952-56. He was replaced by Ted Tubb, but the magazine was always a poor relation of the Nova magazines, and it eventually ceased publication in 1957.

The Scottish SF magazine *Nebula* also owed its existence to the economic opportunism of the post-war paperback boom. Its editor, Peter Hamilton, left school in 1952 just as his parents, who were the proprietors of a small printing firm, were contemplating branching out into publishing in order to keep their machines active while other business was slack. He volunteered to edit a line of SF novels for them, but quickly converted this into a magazine on the advice of his distributor. *Nebula* occupied the idle time of the firm's machines between 1952 and 1959, thus justifying its existence in spite of its negligible profitability.

Scion also decided, when the boom petered out, that a magazine might be a better bet than a line of novels, and they launched the *Vargo Statten Science Fiction Magazine* in 1954. They tried to colonize a new niche in the already-overcrowded field, beginning the magazine as a pulp aimed at juvenile readers. Fearn was not the original editor, but he was installed in that post by the new management when Scion went bust and were taken over. His cramped editorial budget meant that he could only pay half what the competition was offering, and the magazine never really stood a chance. It died after releasing nineteen issues under a number of variant titles in 1956, and Fearn's career died with it. It was difficult by then to remember that he had once been the Great White Hope of British SF, regularly featured on the cover of *Astounding Stories of Super-Science* in the days when F. Orlin Tremaine thought that he was a master of the "thought-variant."

* * * * * * *

By 1960, only the Nova Publications magazines survived as original British publications, alongside the British editions of the leading US digests. Their rivals had all decided that the game were not worth the candle, and from a purely commercial point of view they were absolutely right. The profit to be made from SF magazines was by no means huge, and was far more easily made by reprinting US titles than by maintaining original British ones. On the other hand, the existence of a domestic market did make a big difference to the small community of British SF writers, and was a vital element in sustaining their careers at a time when opportunities for hardcover publication were scarce and paperback publication offered very limited rewards. The Nova magazines were of cardinal importance to the development of such writers as John Brunner, Brian Aldiss and J. G. Ballard, and *Nebula* retains the distinction of having published the first short stories of Aldiss, Bob Shaw, and Robert Silverberg.

Nova Publications was not, in any real sense, a commercial operation. *New Worlds*, *Science Fantasy*, and their eventual companion *Science Fiction Adventures*—a title inherited from a US magazine whose UK edition Nova had taken on before it went bust, and subsequently elected to continue—made enough money to keep Ted Carnell alive, and enabled him to build up the literary agency which subsequently became his main business, but his continuing enthusiasm was such a vital prerequisite for their survival that the company could not survive its eventual waning, and the titles had to be sold.

New Worlds and *Science Fantasy* were acquired by Roberts & Vinter, who appointed Michael Moorcock and

101

Kyril Bonfiglioli as the new editors. Both had radically new ideas about how the magazines could and ought to be transformed in order to bring a new respectability and literary ambition to British SF, freeing it at last from the legacy of ill-repute it had acquired by virtue of its downmarket origins in the post-war boom. (Roberts & Vinter were otherwise quite content to carry on that tradition, becoming the latest promulgators of the multi-faceted career of Hank Janson.) Moorcock—and Bonfiglioli's successors at *Impulse*, Keith Roberts and Harry Harrison—had made a solid beginning when the magazines were killed by the shockwaves generated by the bankruptcy of their distributors, Thorpe & Porter.

It was the demise of Thorpe & Porter which also killed off the UK editions of the US magazines, but the gap which they left was easily and rapidly filled by imported copies of the US editions. It was not so easy to resurrect *New Worlds*, but the boundless enthusiasm of its new editor was equal to the task and *New Worlds* eventually reappeared, partly supported by an Arts Council grant, in a lavish new format. Moorcock's efforts on behalf of the publication were nothing less than Herculean, but they could not in the end maintain its existence in a determinedly hostile world. He might have succeeded in keeping the radically re-modelled magazine going had not the major distributors W. H. Smith and John Menzies refused to circulate it during a pettifogging moral panic about bad language in Norman Spinrad's *Bug Jack Barron*, but that final blow was crippling.

The name *New Worlds* had by then acquired such symbolic meaning that it stubbornly refused to die, but its most recent incarnations—including its present one—have not been magazines. Whether the present version will be able to resist assassination by the logic of the marketplace remains to be seen, but the track record of the many original anthology series which have been optimistically launched during the last 20 years offers little grounds for optimism.

* * * * * * *

So it goes—and so it goes on. Year in and year out new enthusiasts come forward, with missionary fervor, to found new British SF magazines. Somewhere on that economic margin, they feel certain, there must be money to be made—or, if not, there must a least be the opportunity to survive, without losing so much that it will become impossible to continue to serve the cause. And SF is, after all, a cause as well as—or perhaps rather than—a publishing category. Even those who pounded the stuff out in the early '50s for next-to-nothing, with little hope of ever raising themselves from the literary gutter, had stars in their eyes.

Interzone, like all its predecessors and all the other SF magazines—including the so-called "semi-professional" magazines—which exist alongside it, owes its existence to the simple determination of the people who produce it. None of these people draws a living wage; in effect, they pay for the privilege of doing what they do. What they do is important not only to themselves, but to all the people whose work finds an outlet in their pages. The writers who appear in *Interzone* do not make more than a tiny fraction of their income from their sales, but that fraction is more important than the marginal difference it makes to their bank balances; a magazine is a display window, a training ground, and something of which one can be proud to be a part.

Every essay in economic history really ought to end with an explicit acknowledgement of the fact that money is, after all, merely a symbol, and not the only possible or credible system of valuation. It makes the wheels of industry go round, but it cannot determine where the carriage will or ought to go.

As products go, SF has a lot to be said for it: it doesn't kill anybody, it doesn't use up much in the way of non-renewable resources, it doesn't create much waste, it's mostly fun, and it offers food for thought which is occasionally nourishing as well as flavorsome.

There will probably be many more British SF magazines in time to come, but it's highly probable that none of them will ever make any real money. Let's hope that there will always be people who are prepared to produce them anyway. And let's hope that no more Adolf Hitlers will emerge to make thing even worse than they'd otherwise be.

VIII.

THE BATTLE OF DORKING
AND ITS AFTERMATH

The May 1871 issue of *Blackwood's Magazine* caused a political sensation and unleashed a furore of journalistic debate which took several years to die down. The complicated chain of cause-and-effect thus started was eventually to extend into the twentieth century, and to make itself felt in the unfolding of the unprecedented web of events which was dramatically to reshape the social and economic order of the emergent world community: the Great War.

The item which set this snowball effect in train was a novella entitled "The Battle of Dorking: Reminiscences of a Volunteer," which took the form of a story recounted by an old man to his grandchildren, recalling the terrible events of "fifty years ago." At that time, we learn—quickly catching on to the fact that it is the reader's present day—Britain was a great and prosperous power, reaping the economic benefits of a worldwide empire. Unfortunately, her military might had been spread too thin in defending this empire, and the nation was utterly unprepared to meet a sudden declaration of war by one of her (unnamed) European neighbors.

The old man describes the hurried attempt to put together an army of volunteers to meet the army of invasion dispatched by the enemy, and the hopeless attempt by that untrained and ill-equipped company to halt the invaders near Box Hill, close to the town of Dorking. That single terrible event, he now recalls, was responsible for the parlous state into which the nation has fallen in his present day, having

105

suffered catastrophic humiliation and impoverishment. He observes:

> The bitterest part of our reflection is that all this misery and decay might have been so easily prevented, and that we brought it about ourselves by our own shortsighted recklessness. There, across the narrow Straits, was the writing on the wall, but we would not choose to read it.... Power was then passing away from the class which had been used to rule, and to face political dangers...into the hands of the lower classes, uneducated, untrained to the use of political rights, and swayed by demagogues; and the few who were wise in their generation were denounced as alarmists, or as aristocrats who sought their own aggrandizement by wasting public money on bloated armaments.... Truly the nation was ripe for a fall; but when I reflect how a little firmness and self-denial, or political courage and foresight, might have averted the disaster, I feel that the judgement must have really been deserved.[1]

This clever exercise in alarmism was enormously successful. It was quickly reprinted as a sixpenny pamphlet and sold 80,000 copies within a month. It caused such a stir in the political establishment that the Prime Minister, Gladstone, felt obliged to rail against it in a speech delivered on September 2nd, when he bitterly lamented the fact that this exposé of Britain's supposed unreadiness to defend her shores had been read by all her enemies. The story was, of course, a big hit in the newly-consolidated German Empire following its rapid translation; the Germans, like everyone else, assumed that the unnamed enemy was themselves, and that the writing on the wall to which the old man regretfully referred was their spectacularly successful invasion of France and subsequent victory in the Franco-Prussian War.

A political campaign in favor of rearmament and reform of Britain's military forces had been under way for some considerable time, and many articles and pamphlets had already been written to support that cause. European observers who had witnessed the use of many kinds of new military hardware in the American Civil War of 1861-65 had brought back ominous news of the manner in which new technologies would transform the business of warfare, in terms of its logistics as well as the actual fighting. *The Battle of Dorking* spectacularly upstaged all previous exercises in this vein by means of its striking format, and popularized the debate in no uncertain terms. It could hardly have appeared at a more sensitive time; the French had lost Paris to the invading Prussians in January, mere days after Wilhelm I had been proclaimed German Emperor at Versailles, and the bloodily brief reign of the Paris Commune was under way at the time of publication (it extended from the last week in March to the last week in May).

It is hardly surprising that such a milestone in the history of propaganda stimulated a swift and loud response, which included many replies in kind. The full story of the scare is chronicled in some detail in I. F. Clarke's excellent book, *Voices Prophesying War, 1763-1984*, and a comprehensive list of the replies in kind can be found in Clarke's bibliography of *The Tale of the Future*. The Cornmarket reprint of 1972 adds four such replies to the original novella.

* * * * * * *

The author of *The Battle of Dorking* was George Tomkyns Chesney, who was then a forty-one-year-old Captain in the Royal Engineers and brother of the professor of military history at Sandhurst. His subsequent career went from strength to strength; he was promoted to Lieutenant-Colonel in 1874, full Colonel in 1884, and General in 1892. From 1892 until his death in 1895 he was the Tory M.P. for Oxford.

Chesney was to write one further story of imaginary warfare, *The New Ordeal* (1879). It made far less impact, partly because it seemed far less plausible than its predecessor but also because it aimed at constructive optimism rather than exploiting the melodramatic potential of quasi-apocalyptic alarmism. Whereas *The Battle of Dorking* is based in a scrupulously careful estimation of the actual resources of Britain's land forces in 1871, *The New Ordeal* looks forward to an unspecified time when new and more powerful explosives have been developed—an evolution which, Chesney proposes, would make warfare impossible, necessitating its replacement by 105-a-side gladiatorial combats. In a world which has lived with the atom bomb for nearly half a century such naïvety seems rather quaint, but *The New Ordeal* does provide a useful insight into the popular notion of the day that the end of war was, indeed, imminent, and that the next war to be fought might and ought to be the last.

The British tradition of scientific romance which emerged in the newly-fledged popular magazines in the final decade of the nineteenth century owed a great deal to the example of *The Battle of Dorking* and to the vogue for imaginary war stories which Chesney's novella inspired. Although the excitement it generated had long since died down and the flow of exercises in imitation had virtually dried up by 1890, its brief celebrity had by no means been forgotten. When a host of new periodicals was launched in London in the wake of *The Strand*, competing fiercely for the kind of broad middlebrow audience which had long been securely held in Scotland by *Blackwood's*, the publishing coup of May 1871 immediately came to mind.

Admiral Philip Colomb, who had described *The Battle of Dorking* as a "wonderful and stirring romance," roped in three collaborators to help him plan a realistic account of "The Great War of 1892" for serialization in that year in *Black & White*; it was reprinted in book form as *The Great War of 189-* (1893). This earnest epic was, however, quickly upstaged by a much more spectacular account of future war offered in *Pearson's Weekly* by one of C. Arthur Pearson's journalists, George Griffith: *The Angel of the Revolution*.

Griffith imagined an early twentieth-century war being waged by self-styled Terrorists against all the empires of the world, employing new explosives of unprecedented

108

power delivered to their targets by airships and submarines. The Terrorists' campaign leads to the establishment of a World State, but the prize is not cheaply won. The hero of the novel announces in the first chapter that "the next war will be the greatest carnival of destruction the world has ever seen," and once his forces have taken to the air he is quick to observe that the bombing of cities will involve whole populations in war, and that the day of "non-combatants" is done.

Not to be outdone in this escalating conflict, Pearson's great rival Alfred Harmsworth commissioned one of his own journalists, William Le Queux, to provide his periodical *Answers* with an account of *The Great War in England in 1897*. This was reprinted in book form in 1894 with a preface by Field-Marshal Lord Roberts, and went through sixteen editions in the next five years. Tower Books, which reprinted both *The Angel of the Revolution* and *The Great War in England in 1897* in the wake of the naval war story *The Captain of the 'Mary Rose'* (1892) by W. Laird Clowes, went on to publish several more handsomely illustrated books in the same vein. Griffith's illustrator was Fred T. Jane, who went on to found *Jane's Fighting Ships* in 1898 (later to be supplemented by *Jane's Fighting Aircraft* and other similar volumes). Jane wrote a near-future war novel of his own for Tower, *Blake of the 'Rattlesnake'* (1895), which was in the realistic vein of Clowes and Colomb, but his vivid illustrations of giant airships locked in mortal combat were adornments perfectly suited to Griffith's extravaganza.

Griffith followed up *The Angel of the Revolution* with an apocalyptic sequel, *Olga Romanoff* (1894), and a similarly lurid account of *The Outlaws of the Air* (1895), but Pearson was already encouraging others among his employees to turn their hands to this kind of work. Another who did so was Louis Tracy, who produced a fervently militaristic and jingoistic account of *The Final War* (reprinted by Pearson under his own imprint in 1896), which is finally won by Britain, with the aid of "electric rifles," despite the fact that Germany, France, and Russia combine their forces against her and American support is slow and somewhat equivocal. In a brief preface to the book edition Tracy claimed that into the mouths of actual persons he had "placed the finest sentiments I could extract from a nature seared by journalism."

Tracy in his turn was later to encourage the young M. P. Shiel—who had written some chapters of the serial version of *An American Emperor* (1897) for him while he was ill—to produce a similar epic, "The Empress of the Earth," which was reprinted in book form as *The Yellow Danger* (1898). Although Shiel could not bring himself wholeheartedly to support the kind of social Darwinist ideas that Tracy espoused he carried forward his notion of a great clash between West and East for mastery of the world into other novels, most notably *The Dragon* (1913, revised as *The Yellow Peril*), thus—unintentionally—laying the groundwork for the "yellow peril" thrillers of Sax Rohmer. While Tracy followed up *The Final War* with the relatively modest *The Invaders* (1901) Shiel developed his extravagant story of world conquest *The Lord of the Sea* (1901) into a Messianic fantasy.

The futuristic imagery of Griffith's and Shiel's stories make them much more akin to modern works of science fiction than those of their more realistically-inclined contemporaries, and we can now see that Griffith had a clearer idea of the rapidity and likely scope of technological change than most of his rivals, but it was the less imaginatively-adventurous writers who had the best chance of reaching best-seller status. Le Queux's *The Great War in England in 1897* is so meagre in its technical inventions that Darko Suvin declines to list it in the main body of his bibliography of *Victorian Science Fiction in the UK* (1983), relegating it to an appendix of "Books Dealing with Future War and Politics Only," but it was the biggest seller in the 1890s boom. It is hardly surprising that it was Le Queux to whom Alfred Harmsworth turned again in 1905 when he wanted to boost the circulation of his *Daily Mail*—the first popular daily newspaper in England.

Harmsworth commissioned Le Queux to compile a new account of a German invasion of England, which he began to serialize in March 1906. In the course of this invasion the Germans had to pass through virtually every big town in the land, so that their advance could be correlated with a large-scale advertising campaign whose stunts included sandwich-board men in German uniforms marching up and down Oxford Street. The story was reprinted in book form as *The Invasion of 1910* (shortened in editions issued after 1910 to *The Invasion*).

The ground had been prepared for Harmsworth's new endeavor by the spectacular success of a book which was perhaps the biggest best-seller the boom produced: Erskine Childers's *The Riddle of the Sands* (1903). This was an important early example of the "thriller" genre which was to be extensively developed in the next ten years by the spy stories of Le Queux and E. Phillips Oppenheim. The plot describes the discovery by two young Englishmen on a yachting holiday of a German canal-building project which is a key element in their preparations for an invasion of Britain. Many such dastardly schemes were to be discovered and thwarted as the new genre became popular. John Buchan's *The Thirty-Nine Steps* (1914), written in feverish haste during the first weeks of the war while the author's bad health frustrated his fervent ambition to get into the action, quickly became a great favorite in the trenches.

* * * * * * *

The popular attitude to the possibility that Britain might soon be involved in a European war, enshrined in these texts and many others of the same kind, is curiously ambivalent. All of the writers involved were aware of the fact that war was a nasty business, and that technological progress was bringing about a rapid increase in the killing power of modern weapons. On the other hand, all of them felt—or were prepared to suppose for the sake of their stories—that a crucial settlement of European political affairs, particularly concerning the worldwide imperial ambitions of the major European nation-states, was both necessary and inevitable. It was taken for granted by all these works that a new world order was in the making, and that it would almost certainly have to undergo a baptism of fire.

The overwhelming majority of the writers caught up in the boom in future war stories believed—as George Chesney did in 1871—that Britain was in a good position to defeat her major competitors and establish a commanding position in the new world order, if only her military forces could be well enough equipped, but that the cost of failure in this regard would be enormous. The journalists urged by their rival proprietors to outdo one another in capturing the public imagination were, of course, by no means remiss in flattering the patriotic vainglory of their readers, frequently suggesting that it was in fact the destiny of the British people to inherit the earth, provided that they did not seek to do so by meekness.

The most jingoistic of all these texts was Tracy's *The Final War*, whose rousing concluding chapter argues that it was always the destiny of the Anglo-Saxon race to bring about a third great world-empire (succeeding the Greek and Roman), according to the law of the survival of the fittest. This third reich is all the more glorious because it is unassailable, instituting as it does an era of eternal peace—which Tracy, typically, chooses to describe in the terminology of an imaginary newspaper article from the *Newcastle Chronicle*:

> One thrilling thought remains. The cannon has spoken its last word. In all the savage incoherence of its cruel, inarticulate speech it has roared its ghastly message from century to century, writing its meaning in the writhing bodies of its victims, or tracing it along the blackened ruins of fair cities.... But gun and cannon and bayonet and shell are silenced at last. In future ages, when new generations see in their museums these horrid implements, they will indeed wonder that the nineteenth century should have been so self-deluded as to deem itself civilised.[2]

(In fairness, it ought to be noted that modern visitors to the Imperial War Museum may indeed wonder at the delusions of the nineteenth-century militarists—but not quite for the reasons Tracy imagined.)

It is difficult to judge the extent to which the myth of a war to end war penetrated the popular consciousness of the day, but we do know that this was the slogan under which the actual war of 1914-18 was sold to the people who had to support and fight it. Volunteers were summoned forth in their hundreds of thousands to man the trenches in Belgium and France with the promise that they were fighting a war to save civilization and to make the world secure for once and for all. The people who made that promise probably did not realize that it was a foul lie; the people who responded to it certainly did not.

Not everyone, of course, believed in the myth. George Griffith was not prepared to let his awareness of the potential of new military technologies interfere with his enthusiasm for the coming conflict—in his last future war novel, *The Lord of Labour* (posthumously published in 1911), the war is fought with atomic missiles and disintegrator rays but is still presented as a glorious endeavor—but others did perceive that such devices might more easily destroy civilization than save it. In his pioneering work of futurology, *Anticipations* (1901), H. G. Wells cautiously suggested that aircraft would have little impact on twentieth-century warfare, but once the Wright brothers had actually taken off he quickly revised his opinion. In *The War in the Air* (1908) he produced a compelling account of the reversion of society to a quasi-Medieval state as a result of the aerial bombing of the major cities.

Even Wells, however, thought that a certain amount of destruction might be a thoroughly good thing, and might indeed be necessary before a new and better world order could be born out of its ashes. In *The World Set Free* (1914), issued on the eve of the actual Great War, many cities are rendered uninhabitable by atomic bombs whose "chain reactions" cause them to explode repeatedly, but this is merely the prelude to social reconstruction, and is justified on the grounds of painful necessity by the philosopher whose ideas are set forth in the final section of the text.

* * * * * * *

The actual history of the Great War bore little or no resemblance to any of the imaginary wars which were fought in fiction between 1871 and 1914. The world of the 1920s bore little enough resemblance to any new world order anticipated in that fiction, and if Britain's status within the community of nations was not quite as desperate as that described by Chesney's regretful volunteer, it certainly came nowhere near to measuring up to Tracy's high hopes. Many Britons felt that they and the millions recruited as cannon-fodder had been betrayed by their political leaders and military commanders, and most of the men who were recruited to the now-ailing genre of scientific romance in the decades following the end of the great war felt that the Great War had taught speculators an invaluable lesson: that war could not and would not put an end to war, but could and might put an end to civilization.

In general, the writers who had emerged before the war were less extreme in adopting this new perspective than those who had earlier committed themselves to the cause of re-fighting and winning the battle of Dorking and its analogues. Chesney, Colomb, Clowes, and Griffith were all long dead, but William Le Queux, Louis Tracy, H. G. Wells, and M. P. Shiel all survived the war. Neither Le Queux nor Tracy wrote anything to compare with *The Invasion of 1910* or *The Final War*, but neither did they write anything to suggest that they repented of their jingoistic militarism, and Le Queux's thrillers remained as relentlessly xenophobic as they always had been. Wells never abandoned the notion that before the world could achieve a properly ordered state its present institutions would have to be torn down and the power of its defenders smashed; *Men Like Gods* (1923) assumes such a pattern and *The Shape of Things to Come* describes it in bloody detail. Shiel returned to scientific romance only at the end of his life, when he too produced a novel of benign apocalypse, in which dire confusion attends the birth pangs of a braver and better world: *The Young Men Are Coming!* (1937). The work of these writers contrasts strongly with the darkly apocalyptic alarmist novels which flooded from other pens: Edward Shanks's *The People of the Ruins* (1920), Cicely Hamilton's *Theodore Savage* (1922), Shaw Desmond's *Rag-*

narok (1926), Miles's *The Gas War of 1940* (1931, also known as *Valiant Clay* by Neil Bell), John Gloag's *Tomorrow's Yesterday* (1932), Frank McIlraith and Roy Connolly's *Invasion from the Air* (1934), S. Fowler Wright's trilogy concluded with *Megiddo's Ridge* (1937), and Philip George Chadwick's *The Death Guard* (1939).

One writer, though, did begin to wonder about the part which he might have played in contributing to the enthusiasm with which the people of Britain finally went to war with Germany. Erskine Childers, author of *The Riddle of the Sands*, regretted the possibility that his story had helped to rouse anti-German feeling. In his own introductions to later editions of the novel issued before 1914 he took care to welcome the fact that relations between the two nations had improved since he wrote the book, and when it fell to his brother to introduce the edition of 1931, the younger Childers was explicit about his sibling's change of heart:

> In *The Riddle of the Sands*, first published in 1903, Erskine Childers advocated preparedness for war as being the best preventative of war. During the years that followed, he fundamentally altered his opinion. His profound study of military history, of politics, and later of the causes of the Great War convinced him that preparedness induced war. It was not only that to the vast numbers of people engaged in the fostered war services and armament industries, war meant the exercise of their professions and trades and the advancement of their interests; preparedness also led to international armament rivalries, and bred in the minds of the nations concerned fears, antagonisms, and ambitions, that were destructive to peace.[3]

All this was, of course, a long time ago—and we are, after all, only talking about works of fiction. It is difficult to believe nowadays that there is any lesson still to be learned

115

from *The Battle of Dorking* and its strange progeny. Another World War has been fought since then, and we have spent most of our own lifetimes engaged in a "Cold War" in which preparedness for Armageddon supposedly succeeded in preventing Armageddon from actually taking place. Even so, it may be worth recalling now what ultimately became of Erskine Childers, the man who changed his mind.

Winston Churchill—who never wrote an imaginary war story *per se*, but made a highly significant contribution to the ongoing debate with his article "Shall We Commit Suicide?" (1924), which argued passionately that the next war would very probably destroy civilization, and was therefore to be avoided at all costs—produced an epitaph of sorts for Childers when he died in 1922, executed by firing squad after a secret trial, while his appeal was still pending:

> I have seen with satisfaction that the mischief-making murderous renegade Erskine Childers has been captured. No man has done more harm or shown more genuine malice, or endeavored to bring a greater curse on the common people of Ireland than this strange being, actuated by a deadly and malignant hatred for the land of his birth.[4]

This remarkable outburst was occasioned by the fact that from 1914 until his death Erskine Childers had been active in the Irish Republican Army, whose chief propagandist he became. He was a dedicated opponent of partition, believing that the division of Ireland would result in a long-protracted conflict that would prove enormously difficult to resolve.

However difficult it may be to perceive and judge their significance, history and imaginary history, seen in juxtaposition, are not without their little ironies.

IX.

THE SCIENCE IN SCIENCE FICTION

The kind of fiction which we nowadays call "science fiction" first became popular a little more than a hundred years ago. Before that time the great majority of people were hardly aware of the march of technological progress. They thought of social change mostly in terms of politics and wars: as a series of temporary disturbances of the basic routines of life. In the course of the last century, though, it became obvious to large numbers of people that new technologies were transforming the world dramatically, at such a fast pace that enormous changes might now be expected to take place within the space of a single human lifetime. As that awareness spread, it was entirely natural that stories which made guesses about the kinds of change which would take place became more popular.

The nineteenth-century inventions which made the most significant differences to the patterns of human life were those affecting the productivity of factories and farms and those connected with the growth of scientific medicine, but the new machines which had the most dramatic effect on the imagination of popular writers were those which revolutionized leisure and tourism—particularly new means of transportation, like the railway locomotive and the steamship. It was this kind of inspiration which led Jules Verne, the first great popular writer of science fiction, to write a long series of accounts of "extraordinary voyages" in which he dispatched his characters to every remote part of the world's surface, and various destinations beyond. His best-known works include *A Journey to the Centre of the Earth*

(1864), *From the Earth to the Moon* (1865) and its sequel *Round the Moon* (1870), and *Twenty Thousand Leagues Under the Sea* (1873).

Verne always tried to be scrupulously realistic in his use of science. His most adventurous novels are crammed with technical details—although his British publishers, aiming at a younger audience, often took a lot of it out. He was, however, forced to gloss over the detailed workings of his as-yet-uninvented machines and he was understandably prone to make the odd mistake. For example, his account in *Twenty Thousand Leagues Under the Sea* of how the submarine *Nautilus* draws electrical power directly from the seawater around it is necessarily vague, while the diving suits described in the text would be fatal to their users because they are not properly pressurized.

Verne's imitators were mostly far less conscientious in their description of imaginary technology than he was. For instance, his sometime collaborator Paschal Grousset (who wrote his fiction under the pen-name André Laurie) produced a novel called *The Conquest of the Moon* (1888) in which the difficulties of travelling through the vacuum which separates the Earth from the moon are avoided by using gigantic magnets to draw the moon into the atmosphere for a while—a notion which pays little heed to the niceties of the theory of gravity. The English writer John Mastin, who took great care to list all his degrees and other scientific qualifications in the by-line which he used on his Vernian romances, was nevertheless perfectly happy to entertain extreme improbabilities in his novels, which include the aptly-titled *Through the Sun in an Airship* (1909).

Many people were quick to realize that new kinds of transportation would not merely transform the business of tourism but also the business of war, and some took to writing alarmist fantasies to alert others to the danger. Sir George Chesney's account of a German invasion of Britain which succeeds by virtue of the German army's use of advanced equipment, *The Battle of Dorking* (1871), became a best-seller not only in Britain but also—more worryingly—in Germany. Verne, for the sake of dramatic plotting, had placed his imaginary submarine, the *Nautilus*, in the hands of

118

the enigmatic pirate Captain Nemo, who uses it to mount sneak attacks on the ships of nations he disapproves of (particularly Britain). When he eventually wrote a story about an airship, *The Clipper of the Clouds* (1886), he put it at the disposal of a man with even greater dreams of conquest, who aspires to become—as the title of the sequel has it—the *Master of the World*.

Future war stories, usually featuring invasions by France or Germany, became very popular in Britain as the nineteenth century neared its end. The weapons used in such imaginary wars grew more and more spectacular. George Griffith began his career as a novelist in 1893 with *The Angel of the Revolution*, an account of a war waged by heroic Terrorists against all the tyrants of the world, using airships, submarines, and new explosives to rain destruction upon combatants and civilians alike. At the time of his death, only thirteen years later, he was working on a novel in which the heroic defenders of Britain are able to deploy tactical nuclear weapons fired from bazookas against enemies who are armed with disintegrator rays which reduce ironclad ships to dust in a matter of minutes. The unexpected discovery of X-rays by Röntgen had by this time inspired science fiction writers to devise countless new kinds of rays, some of which could work all manner of medical miracles, but most of which simply wrought destruction on a grand scale.

A good deal of modern science fiction still deals with hi-tech crimes and ultra-destructive wars, but this is not because science fiction writers have viewed technology as something essentially nasty. It has much more to do with the fact that the peaceful and productive uses of technology don't make very exciting reading. Good stories require lots of action, dire threats and spectacular nick-of-time escapes. For this reason, science fiction mostly shows technology at its most menacing, whereas futurology—non-fiction about the march of progress—tends to show it in a much more benign light. Stories about new inventions almost always show the machines going wrong, or describe how their use gives rise to unexpectedly awkward or horrific consequences; if they didn't, there wouldn't be any story to tell. Science fiction stories, like Spanish holiday resorts, might be entertain-

119

ing places to visit briefly, but no one in his right mind would want to live in one.

The most outstanding of the early British writers of science fiction, H. G. Wells, took an intensely serious interest in the potential of technology to change the world for the better, and he wrote several Utopian fantasies about ideal states of the future, but readers have always preferred his more melodramatic scientific romances, which include the mad scientist stories *The Island of Dr Moreau* (1896) and *The Invisible Man* (1897) and the first novel about an alien invasion of Earth, *The War of the Worlds* (1898). Many people regret that Wells gave up writing such melodramas soon after the turn of the century in order to concentrate on more earnest concerns.

Wells was initially compared by readers and reviewers to Verne, but Verne reacted strongly against such comparisons. "I make use of science," he once told an interviewer, indignantly, "he invents." Verne went on to argue that the space gun used in *Round the Moon* was a plausible means of firing a capsule into orbit, while the gravity-defying metal Cavorite which is used as a means of transport by *The First Men in the Moon* (1901) was pure fantasy. Later writers have argued about the justice of this claim—Verne's space gun would inflict terrible injuries on any passengers reckless enough to ride inside the missiles which it fires, and some modern commentators have suggested that a gravity screen might not be such a silly idea as Verne thought—but disputes about the relative practicality of the two devices miss the point. Wells didn't care one way or the other whether Cavorite really was a likely discovery, as long as it could be made to sound plausible; what he wanted was a way of getting his characters to the moon so that they could meet the Selenites and see how an alien society might work. Wells was the first writer fully to appreciate that imaginary machines which were quite impossible could nevertheless be very useful assistants in the cause of careful and constructive speculation. He had already demonstrated this point in the first of his long scientific romances, *The Time Machine*, which introduced a key example of a hypothetical machine used purely as a "facilitating device"—which is to say, as a way of easing the flight of the imagination.

Although the hero of *The Time Machine* (1895) gives a long lecture to his listeners regarding the scientific theory according to which the time machine is supposed to work, the argument is a mere smokescreen of jargon. Wells invented a time machine not because he thought that such a machine could ever be invented, but simply because it was so very useful as a means of allowing his hero to investigate the entire evolutionary future of mankind. Once granted the single premise of the machine, Wells was then extremely scrupulous about trying to map out a plausible future history for mankind and life on earth. Other writers were, of course, quick to see he potential he had opened up. Time machines became one of the staple devices of science fiction, widely employed to visit the past as well as the future—the age of the dinosaurs quickly became a favorite destination.

Like Verne before him, Wells made understandable mistakes in depicting the likely shape of the future in *The Time Machine*. The scientists of the day, knowing nothing about nuclear fusion, thought that the sun's heat was produced by burning, and Wells was therefore completely wrong about its likely lifetime and eventual fate. Nevertheless, the extrapolations set out in *The Time Machine* do take aboard the most advanced scientific ideas of its day. At other times, Wells was quite prepared to cheat; unlike many of the writers who came after him he realized that if light passed straight through an invisible man, uninterrupted by the retina of the eye, the world around him would be just as invisible to him as he was to it, but Wells was prepared to ignore that inconvenient fact for the sake of his story. In spite of such lapses, though, he was a writer who took the business of futuristic speculation very seriously, and he used his science fiction stories cleverly to develop earnest arguments about the way the world might be and perhaps ought to be going.

Science fiction has always made extravagant use of facilitating devices like the time machine and Cavorite. Almost all sciencefictional spaceships fit into this category. Jules Verne's characters could only take a trip around the moon, because he had no way to get them back into space if they landed, but other writers were not prepared to entertain such awkward limitations. They were perfectly ready to fudge the issue of how spaceships could be powered and how they might be designed, just so long as they could take off and land with a minimum of fuss. Taking such things for granted allowed them to get on with the much more interesting business of describing what life on other worlds might be like. People had been writing about trips to the moon and Mars for centuries before Konstantin Tsiolkovsky first proposed that the sensible way to get out into space was to use rockets (an idea frivolously anticipated by the French writer Cyrano de Bergerac, nowadays remembered only for the size of his nose) and many writers continued to refuse to be bothered with anything so dull and awkward. Antigravity devices and mysterious atomic motors were so much more convenient.

As time went by, the design of science fictional spaceships had to become even more extravagant. The more astronomers found out about the actual conditions on the other worlds of the solar system, the less promising those worlds seemed as settings for exciting adventure stories. One can see this very clearly in the evolution of fictional images of Mars, which progress from the lushly exotic locales of Edgar Rice Burroughs's *A Princess of Mars* (1912) and its sequels through the nostalgic dying-world scenarios of Ray Bradbury's *Martian Chronicles* (1950) to the grim post-Mariner realism of Kim Stanley Robinson's novel *Red Mars* (1992). Because of the gradual wasting of this fictional resource it became necessary for science fiction writers to find ways of getting to other stars, which could easily be equipped with Earthlike worlds in limitless abundance. In order to do this it was convenient to pretend that Einstein's theory of general relativity—which rules that faster-than-light travel is logically inconceivable—is a minor obstacle easily overcome by means of some kind of "overdrive" or "space warp," or by ducking into "hyperspace." Nowadays the favorite device is to use hyperspatial tunnels associated with black holes, and modern science fiction writers slickly skate over the vital question of how a spaceship and its crew might actually be able to get into a black hole without being crushed into a mere blob of superdense matter in the process.

The use of these kinds of imaginary technologies is unashamed cheating, but the deployment of such literary devices is by no means incompatible with serious and scrupulous attempts to describe what life on another world might actually be like. Usually it turns out to be broadly similar to, but in some significant way different from, life on Earth. Science fiction writers are often very conscientious in mapping out the logical consequences of such differences, whether they occur at the physical, biological or social level. There is, of course, a good deal of science fiction which only uses machines as facilitating devices—in what are sometimes called "space operas" by false analogy with "soap operas" huge and heavily-armed starships are used mainly to fight spectacular battles—but such devices also have a crucial role to play in the so-called "hard science fiction" which involves serious scientific extrapolation.

Matter transmitters are another popular species of facilitating device, whose utility is readily demonstrated in every episode of *Star Trek* in which the crudely-named "transporter" is used as a convenient means of ship-to-shore travel. The transporter is equally convenient to *Star Trek*'s script-writers as a way of magically whisking the lead characters out of tight situations—a resource which they sometimes overuse as a means of moving the plot along.

Some facilitating devices have come to seem so silly to modern readers as to have lost their fashionability; the once-popular "translation machine," which saved generations of starfaring Earthmen the bother of learning alien languages, is now considered so highly improbable as to be ridiculous. Douglas Adams parodied its use in *The Hitch-Hiker's Guide to the Galaxy*, where space-travellers can avoid the difficulties inherent in trying to understand aliens simply by sticking Babel fish in their ears.

On the other hand, some facilitating devices have generated whole subspecies of science fiction. It is fairly easy to see that the irresponsible use of a time machine could create logical paradoxes. The point is often dramatized by asking what would happen if you were to go back in time and shoot your grandfather before he married your grand-mother, thus eliminating your father—and presumably your-self—from the scheme of things. Rather than accepting this as a conclusive proof of the impossibility of time travel, science fiction writers have enthusiastically produced hundreds of ingenious stories which set out to provide amusing answers to this conundrum, and which delight in tying intricate knots in the pattern of cause and effect. The most notable example is perhaps Robert Heinlein's story "All You Zombies..." (1959), whose lead character flips back and forth in time, undergoing a sex-change in the process, in order to become his own father and mother. "I know where I came from," he says at the end, "but where did all you zombies come from?" This kind of science fiction is a kind of intellectual play, involving clever conjuring tricks with ideas. Although they have nothing to do with practical technologies or possible futures, such stories can be very useful as a way of exercising the imagination.

In the midst of all this game-playing, however, there remains a good deal of modern science fiction which does attempt to exercise the serious art of technological extrapolation: to foresee how today's science might be turned into tomorrow's technology, and how new technologies might transform the world in which we live. Very few of today's technologies were entirely unanticipated in science fiction, and in a handful of cases the visions of science fiction have played a significant role in inspiring the work of scientists. Once Konstantin Tsiolkovsky had published his work on rocketry, and written a science fiction novel of his own to popularize it, many other writers carried the idea forward, thus becoming important agents of propaganda for the development of actual space rockets. The members of a German amateur scientific society were commissioned to design and build a rocket for use in Fritz Lang's film *The Girl in the Moon*, and although they never managed to get it off the ground several of them went on to work at Peenemunde on the V-2 rocket-bomb, and then in the American space pro-gramme. Several British SF writers were active in the British Interplanetary Society, most famously Arthur C. Clarke, whose proposals for the development of communication satellites were first published in an article in *Wireless World* in 1945.

Science fiction also anticipated the advent of nuclear weapons and power plants. The most enthusiastic editors of the early American science fiction magazines, Hugo Gernsback and John W. Campbell Jr., were both convinced that technologies of nuclear fission were just around the corner, and they were very enthusiastic about the possibility. Campbell's articles on the progress of atomic research inspired a whole series of technically-detailed stories about nuclear power and possible atomic weapons. These included such tersely realistic near-future stories as Robert Heinlein's "Blowups Happen" (1940) and Lester del Rey's "Nerves" (1942), the latter describing the desperate attempt to control the potentially-catastrophic consequences of an accident at a nuclear power station situated in a heavily-populated area.

The business of science-fictional extrapolation is not a simple matter of identifying possible technological applications of scientific knowledge, and this is why science fiction is significantly different from futurology. In fiction it is never sufficient simply to describe a new invention; it is also necessary, in order that a story may be told, to describe the world in which the invention is made, and to show how that world might be changed by the invention. It hardly needs to be said that it is very difficult to design a whole world different from our own, whether it be an imaginary future, an alien planet, or an alternative world which might have come into being had some crucial event in history happened otherwise. When the results can be checked out, as is the case when antique science fictional images of the future can be compared to the actual course of history, there is rarely much resemblance between image and actuality. But the fact that the real world of 1984 was very different from that imagined in George Orwell's novel *Nineteen Eighty-Four* does not mean that the world of the novel should be regarded as a mere mistake, or that its production was pointless.

Science fiction writers have generally been cleverer in anticipating the advent of new kinds of machinery than they have in figuring out the roles which such machines would come to play in human society. For example, science fiction stories about robots—which have been around for a hundred years, although the word robot was only coined by Karel Capek in 1922—almost always imagine machines made in the image of men; only a handful of stories dealt with the more specialized kinds of robots which are now commonplace in factories—and those which did, like Claude Farrère's *Useless Hands* (1920), foresee apocalyptic consequences following the displacement of manual laborers by artificial hands. Similarly, science fiction stories about "artificial brains" almost always imagined that the more powerful computers became the more gigantic they would become. Mechanical brains the size of cities, or even the size of planets, became commonplace in science fiction of the '40s and '50s, and almost all of them developed awesome delusions of godlike grandeur. In the meantime, no one at all wrote fiction about a world beset and transformed by a vast profusion—and confusion—of desktop personal computers. This inability to place imaginary technologies within accurate visions of future society is sometimes seen as a crucial failure of science fiction, but that is to take an overly narrow view of what science fiction writers can and ought to do.

We must remember that the world which has actually come into being as a result of the scientific discoveries of the last century is only one of countless worlds which might have come into being in its stead. The failure of science fiction stories about robots and computers as mere prophecies does not mean that the hopes and anxieties reflected in such stories were or are unjustified; nor does it mean that the arguments conducted in such stories were or are irrelevant. One can, and perhaps should, argue that the most useful visions of the future are not those which turn out to be the most accurate, but rather those which alarm people sufficiently to make them act in order to avert the possibilities they describe. In this view, the best images of the future are those which prevent themselves coming true by issuing warnings which are convincing enough to be heeded. At least two science fiction novels—Aldous Huxley's *Brave New World* (1932) and George Orwell's *Nineteen Eighty-Four* (1949)—have had a profound effect on real attitudes to certain social, political and technological trends, and they

126

have done so by playing upon people's anxieties rather than by issuing accurate predictions.

The best of modern science fiction includes, alongside and beneath its purely playful aspects, an ongoing series of discussions about the pros and cons of various emergent or as-yet-uninvented technologies. Current hot topics of concern include information technology, genetic engineering and virtual reality, while old standards like the extension of the human lifespan are continually subject to ever-more-careful re-examination. By the same token, contemporary science fiction continues to issue dire warnings against the possible evil consequences of various well-set historical trends: the population explosion, environmental pollution, the possible exhaustion of natural resources, and so on. In addressing such issues, science fiction writers make use of a whole armory of argumentative weapons, ranging from graphic horror to farcical black comedy.

Even when science fiction deals with highly unlikely eventualities, it often addresses serious issues. Science-fictional robots, as I have pointed out, bear little or no resemblance to the real thing, but science fiction stories which raise questions about whether or not humanoid robots might have feelings, or to what extent they should have legal rights, often bear significantly on the question of what we can or ought to mean by the word "human." Science fiction stories about artificial intelligence—of which there are many—may indeed anticipate actual technological achievements, but they also constitute an interesting and important series of discussions about what such ideas as "intelligence" and "self-consciousness" really involve.

There are, of course, countless science fiction stories about alien beings which raise similar questions about the nature of humanity and intelligence, and man's place in the universe. Such questions are implicit in H. G. Wells's *The War of the Worlds* and *The First Men in the Moon*, and remain central even to such futuristic costume-dramas as *Star Trek*. Many of the science fiction stories which deal with the subjects of alien intelligence and alien ecology also make up a vast series of meditations on the implications of the Darwinian theory of evolution. Whether or not we ever make contact with any real alien beings, this fictional exploration of possibilities is by no means useless as a way of trying to get a clearer sight of our own nature and the evolutionary processes which produced us. We cannot properly understand what we are, and what we might yet make of ourselves, unless we can carefully compare and contrast ourselves with all the things that the processes of evolution might have made of us.

At its most elementary, science fiction is simply fiction which borrows ideas from science and technology, whether it does so in order to anticipate future developments or purely for fun. But the best science fiction does embrace a kind of scientific thinking, and provides a way of exploring certain aspects of scientific theories; in this way science fiction can be a partner of science rather than a mere parasite upon its skin. It is a pity that a great deal of modern science fiction is extremely careless in its use of scientific ideas, and that a great many readers and writers are not sufficiently well-educated in science to perceive its errors or recognize cheating, but at least one may hope that an interest in the wonders of science fiction will help to encourage in those readers an interest in the real possibilities of science and technology.

X.

THE SIREN SONG OF SEXUALITY: THE MYTHOLOGY OF *FEMMES FATALES*

The sirens, half-bird and half-woman, lived on the island of Anthemöessa. Opinions differ as to whether they numbered two or three, or whether their songs were accompanied by musical instruments, but there is unanimity as to the nature of their song: it drove men mad, causing them to lose their memories of wives and children, hearth and home. Deprived of their will to resist, the luckless sailors who heard the sirens sing would plunge into the water and swim towards the isle; many never reached it, and those who did lay listless upon the shore, utterly bewitched, until they wasted away. The shores of Anthemöessa shone white in the sunlight, littered as they were with bleached bones.

* * * * * * *

Such is the myth of the *femme fatale* in its elementary form. She is irresistibly attractive; the intoxication of her presence over-rides all other loves, all dutiful obligations and every instinct of self-preservation. Those who follow her lure are lost, and are usually doomed to ignominious extinction.

Two heroes, having been forewarned by rumor, did contrive to avoid destruction by the sirens. The Argo steered past their isle because Orpheus fought fire with fire, drowning out their song with the equally powerful music of his lyre. Odysseus was even cleverer, and also more ambitious;

he stopped the ears of his crewmen with wax, so that they could not hear the song, and had himself securely bound to the mast of his ship, so that he would be able to hear it without being able to respond. Ironically enough, this ruse was suggested to him by another *femme fatale* of his acquaintance, the sorceress Circe. He had escaped her clutches quite easily, exerting a greater attractive force upon her than she could exert upon him.

Circe forsook her own power to captivate men when she fell in love with Odysseus; such a reversal of fortune is the prescribed path by which *femmes fatales*, may seek and sometimes find redemption. The irredeemable tend to find a different destiny, exemplified by the fate of the sirens. They, following their failure to entrap Odysseus, were bound by an ancient curse to fling themselves into the sea and drown. Temptresses who cannot resign themselves to become dull wives only thrive until that fateful moment comes when they lose their glamour.

* * * * * * *

The *femme fatale* is one of the most ancient mythical motifs, but she is sometimes hidden away, banished to the borderlands of folklore in order that socially-sanctioned images of woman-as-wife and woman-as-mother may take centre stage. Official morality necessarily disapproves of the power which women have to infatuate men, because that power is a threat to the marriage contract which is one of the fundamental pillars of social order.

Official morality in all cultural traditions must come to terms with the untamability of erotic attraction one way or another; the Judaeo-Christian tradition which produced modern Western values took the path of forthright opposition. The principal weapons deployed in this war were vilification and taboo, and the guiding strategy was demonization. That is how the power of female sexuality became imaginatively incarnate in the figure of the *femme fatale*: a creature to be feared and avoided because the mere sight or sound of her is enough to obliterate other loyalties and obligations. The *femme fatale* is frequently represented as a witch or a vampire: as a mistress of black magic or a frankly supernatural being. Either way, her sexual magnetism is held to be unnatural, and her embrace injurious.

The acute discomfort which the official myth-makers of our own cultural tradition felt when confronted with the "problem" of female sexuality is nowhere more evident than in the history of Adam's lost wife, Lilith. Genesis (Chapter 1, verse 27) describes the creation of man, observing that "male and female created he them," and yet Chapter 2 finds Adam alone for some considerable time before God takes pity on his loneliness and forges Eve out of one of his ribs. Apocryphal legend reconciles the two passages by explaining that Adam's first consort was Lilith, who rebelled against the role allotted to her by the Creator and fled from Eden borne aloft by wings which she had conjured up by magic.

Lilith's rebellion cost her dear; angels sent to bring her back warned her that if she would not accept subordination she would be accursed, and that all her children would die in infancy. Still she refused, and became instead the consort of the demon Samael, but she was deeply embittered by her treatment. Her fury and frustration made her the relentless enemy of all the newborn children of her successor, who frequently needed charms to ward her off.

Lilith's obliteration from the orthodox faith of Christianity was completed in the Authorized Version when the sole remaining citation of her name (in Isaiah 34:14) was dismissively translated as "screech-owl." (The Latin Vulgate uses "Lamia," a generic term for female demons which is usually used nowadays—thanks to the popularising activities of Philostratus, Robert Burton and John Keats—to refer to vampiric shape-shifting spirits which can manifest themselves as beautiful women or snakes). She survived nevertheless in oral tradition, and made a triumphant reappearance in Medieval Christian mythology, by which time she had been elevated by some writers to the status of Satan's mistress and Queen of Hell. She was rumored to be the presiding genius of the succubi, female demons sent to earth to wring semen from righteous men by visiting them in lurid dreams, and she was given a key role in the Faust legend, as the se-

ductress whose charms compounded and corrupted the doctor's idealistic quest for knowledge with unholy lust.

The replacement of the carnal and unsubmissive Lilith by the modest and acquiescent Eve—of mistress by
wife—represents the domestication of the sexual impulse by
society. But that victory could never be complete; it is not
only the subsequent history of Lilith which testifies to the
fact, but also the fate of Eve. The harmonious relationship
which Adam and Eve initially share lasts only as long as it
takes for sex to rear its ugly head. Eve is cast in the role of
corrupter; she it is who is tempted by the phallic serpent to
taste the fruit of the tree of knowledge of good and evil, and
she in turn tempts Adam. Having accepted her subordinate
position within their relationship, she is forced also to take
the blame for their fall from grace. In order that she be able
to play the part of dutiful wife and mother, there must of necessity be a little of the glamour of Lilith in her, for which
she and all her female descendants are required to feel eter-
nally guilty. Such is the logic of ideological warfare.

* * * * * * *

The stories of Lilith and Eve demonstrate that the social contract underlying the Western cultural tradition is
awkwardly loaded; buried somewhere in the fine print is a
clause which says that no matter what they do, women cannot win. The reason that they cannot win, of course, is that
the demands which the contract makes of them are con-
tradictory: *femmes fatales* are damned for not being wifely
enough, wives for not being sufficiently *fatale*.

All the kinds of social order that have so far mani-
fested themselves within the Judaeo-Christian tradition (and
perhaps all other kinds of social order) are founded in the
marriage tie, which determines patterns of responsibility and
patterns of inheritance, and that tie must somehow be made
secure. Adulterous desires pose a significant threat to social
order, and if they cannot be accommodated by everyday mo-
res they must be subject to stringent prohibition. Christianity—like the other bargain basement religions, which set out
to win converts by promising salvation in return for rigorous

virtue and Hell as the wages of sin—went for stringent prohibition. But it is one thing to legislate against an act; it is quite another to legislate against an emotion.

Sexual arousal is not entirely subject to the authority of conscious control. It is something which can happen whether a human being wills it or not. Moreover, in the male of the species arousal is clearly stigmatized; it cannot be denied. Despite the immensely useful invention of clothing, which helps to conceal the fact of arousal from witnesses, males cannot deny the experience of sexual arousal, and cannot help but know how feebly their desire is constrained by the bounds of marital legitimacy. The male of the species, continually embarrassed by the taboo-breaking inclinations of his unruly member, is inevitably tempted to shift the blame—and the stronger the taboos which confront him are, the stronger that temptation will become. If he has been reared in the Judaeo-Christian tradition, the temptation is likely to be overwhelming, and blame-shifting the strategy is openly sanctioned by the holy scriptures.

"I couldn't help it," he will say. "It was her fault; she tempted me."

This is, of course, a stupid and hypocritical excuse. It is dishonest and it is cowardly. But males of the species generally have the power to make such slanders stick, if the incentive is strong enough.

Females suffer from wayward sexual arousal too, but their situation is different even at the physical level. Arousal in females is more easily concealed, and hence more easily denied. It is easier for females to pretend—perhaps even to themselves—that they are not really carnal by nature. Anyway, women generally do not have the power to attribute blame where none really belongs; hypocrisy and dishonesty can only become blatant when backed by the kind of authority which defies contradiction.

The idea of the *femme fatale* is one of the products of this blame-shifting facility. In our cultural tradition the woman who tempts the man to forget his contractually-bound social responsibilities is not often permitted merely to be the hapless victim of his overactive hormones; she is frequently charged instead with being a demon or a witch exerting some evil supernatural force upon him. This too is an imaginative move which smacks of self-justificatory exaggeration. (Surely it could not have been the widow who lives over the hill who seduced True Thomas away from his vocation for seven long years, which flew by so quickly that they seemed but a single night? No, of course not—it must have been the Queen of the Fairies!)

In some instances the object of desire is let off this hook because the blame is shifted again, in whole or in part, to the wife of the "victim," whose own powers of attraction are adjudged to be fading, and who might, therefore have trapped him in the first place by means of some temporary charm or spell whose moral propriety must now be doubted. In either case, though, the situation is grim and the prognosis pessimistic. Somebody—perhaps everybody—is going to suffer.

Such is the legacy of the men—they must have been men—who invented the story of Adam and Eve, and exiled Lilith (with extreme prejudice) from the official record.

* * * * * * *

Given all this, it is hardly surprising that when we consult the literary record of our culture we discover that it features two distinct kinds of ideal love.

The first is the social ideal. This is the kind of love which exists, or is supposed to exist, within marriage; it is essentially dutiful, and usually calm. There is no great sexual tension in married love simply because sexual intercourse is fully integrated into the relationship; lust can normally be assuaged as soon as it is aroused.

This kind of ideal love is intrinsically undramatic, and rarely recommends itself to literary celebration except as a goal to be won at last; the vast majority of run-of-the-mill love stories come to an end when a commitment to this kind of relationship has been made, all the dramatic potential created by the initial arousal thus being released. Tolstoy, in the first line of *Anna Karenina*, writes off this kind of love with the casual observation that "all happy marriages are alike" before instantly turning his lascivious contemplation to the

134

heartache which can spring from marriages which fail to meet the standard, every single one of which he holds to be uniquely interesting.

The other kind of ideal love is essentially anti-social. This is the grand passion, born of and based in frustrated arousal; it is essentially spontaneous, and powerfully intoxicating. Sexual tension is intrinsic to this kind of love, which is for that very reason difficult to sustain indefinitely. In order for grand passion to endure, the pressure of lust must either be permanently unrelieved or obsessively renewed. For this reason, this second kind of ideal love may easily be reckoned a delusionary snare—a purely hypothetical ideal imaginatively extrapolated from the feelings associated with arousal—or a kind of mental aberration, a neurotic *idée fixe*.

It is entirely natural that in spite of its evident disadvantages, men should retain a profound respect for the second kind of ideal love, and deem it in some ways more precious than the first; it is, after all, hopelessly impractical. (Whatever is practically attainable is easily taken for granted, even by those who never quite contrive to attain it; whatever is imaginable but forever out of reach always retains its power to fascinate.)

Tranquil contemplation of the second kind of ideal love may easily inspire a certain bitterness, after the celebrated pattern noted by Aesop's fable of the fox and the grapes, but it can also nurture a warm and lachrymose sentimentality. The simple fact that men continue to be capable of spontaneous arousal in spite of every ideological move they make to constrain, or explain, or shift the blame for it, ensures that many of them cannot help but retain their passionate regard for their *femmes fatales* while whatever passionate regard they once had for their wives is patiently eroded by time and familiarity. This occasions in some men a particular kind of melancholy which is uniquely bittersweet.

The idea of grand passion as a form of unfortunate folly verging on outright madness is, of course, familiar to us by courtesy of the mythology and the literature of the Greeks, which the Western World inherited along with all the other detritus of the Alexandrian and Roman Empires. The attitudes of the Greeks to sexual matters were somewhat different to those enshrined in the Judaeo-Christian tradition, their myth-makers having followed the strategy of accommodation rather than that of opposition. The continued influence of Classical ideas upon scholarly men has helped to increase the confusion and ambivalence which is frequently seen in literary treatments of the *femme fatale*; Circe and the sirens are far less demonic than Lilith, and can become interestingly ambiguous when seen from a viewpoint which partakes of both Classical and Christian attitudes.

Ironically, but perhaps inevitably, it was the Christian world which eventually produced a version of grand passion which sought to excuse it from being reckoned either foolish or insane, seeking to defuse its disruptive power by representing it as something potentially noble and sacred. The myth of courtly love first popularized by the troubadours of the twelfth and thirteenth centuries argued that a grand passion, indefinitely sustained by virtue of its careful non-consummation, might—if properly handled—become a fountainhead of virtuous inspiration. The idea was widely touted that a knight's love for his liege-lord's wife, provided always that it remained a chaste and unspoken adoration from a discreet distance, might increase his devotion to the lord and to his knightly duties. This attempted accommodation of the notion of grand passion within the ideology of chivalry was to cast a literary shadow every bit as confused as that cast by Classical representations.

That grand passion has and always has had relatively little effect on the conduct of real life is easily demonstrated by consulting the works of serious historians, who very rarely need to refer to it in order to explain the actions of men of the past. The situation in literature is very different, because literature's primary concern is the dramatic and the routines of social order are inherently undramatic; any sensible definition or explanation of what we mean by the word "dramatic" is forced to refer to the threatened or actual breakdown of social order. For this reason, there is nothing more dramatic than grand passion. As has already been noted, it is Anna Karenina's adulterous passion which makes her a fit subject for literary consideration; had she been happily married there would have been nothing to attract the interest of Tolstoy or anyone else. Similarly, it is the fact that Tristan's love for Isolde, and Lancelot's for Guinevere, tried so very hard to pass, but ultimately failed, the test of chaste containment which fits them for the role of tragic heroes in literature.

In the real world, *femmes fatales* are rare, and whenever a candidate for that status emerges she is quickly shifted from the realm of history to the realm of legend. The reality is immediately obscured, and soon completely obliterated, by the glamour of the myth. There was a real Cleopatra, but she has been comprehensively eclipsed by the mythical Cleopatra; nor is it simply her antiquity which has allowed this to happen. Even in the modern world, attempts by historians to rescue the actual, tawdry, ineffectual Mata Hari from the cloak of mystique with which the forces of rumor and anecdote instantly draped her were always doomed to fail.

The gulf between reality and supernatural literature is, of course, even more exaggerated than that between reality and mundane fiction. It is in literary fantasy that the delusory aspect of grand passion really comes into its own, because the imaginative extrapolation of hypothetical ideals to their logical (or illogical) limit is there permissible. In fantastic fiction the force of grand passion can be given literal supernatural force and sexual arousal can be literally magical. Passion can easily be credited with the power to defy the bounds of everyday reality.

In mundane fiction, grand passion can have only two outcomes: it can be domesticated, decaying into mere married love; or it can lead inexorably to stark tragedy. (The latter is, of course, the preferred outcome in purely aesthetic terms, although there do exist readers so addicted to happy endings that they would rather have seen Romeo and Juliet married than dead.) Fantastic fiction, by contrast, offers the opportunity to discover more exotic escape-routes from this dilemma, as well as the opportunity to remake—and perhaps correct—the myths and legends which embody our attitudes to sexuality. In fantastic literature, the vaguely supernatural quality with which the mundane *femme fatale* is uneasily imbued can be brought into sharp and explicit focus, and completely unfettered. It is through the medium of supernatural fiction that literary men can attempt to come to terms with the essence and the archetype of the *femme fatale*.

* * * * * * *

The modern literary history of the *femme fatale* begins with the Romantic Movement. The Romantics—diehard champions of the emotions against the intellect—took it upon themselves to undertake a sceptical re-evaluation of received ideas of evil, and their sympathy for grand passion inevitably produced numerous accounts of *femmes fatales* which interrogated all aspects of the idea. Even before the advent of the Romantics some such reappraisal had begun in France, as exemplified by Jacques Cazotte's remarkable short novel *Le Diable amoureux* (1772, translated as *The Devil in Love*), where the demonic seductress Biondetta evidently fascinates the author as much as the hero, and is far from being a spirit of pure malevolence.

In the horror stories whose production the Romantic Movement greatly encouraged the *femme fatale* often does appear as a straightforward force of evil. The seductress Matilda in Matthew Gregory Lewis's *The Monk* (1796) is a cardinal example, as is the central character of Goethe's necrophiliac ballad "Die Braut von Korinth" (1798, translated as "The Bride of Korinth"), and the vampiric succubus in Charles Nodier's *Smarra, ou les démons de la nuit* (1820). The image is much more ambiguous, however, in the phantasmagoric and quasi-allegorical horror stories of Ernst Hoffmann, including "Der Goldene Topf" (1813, translated as "The Golden Flower-Pot") and "Der Sandmann" (1816, translated as "The Sandman"), and John Keats's poems "La Belle Dame Sans Merci" and "Lamia" (both 1820). The *femme fatale* became a viewpoint character, treated entirely sympathetically—as an unfortunate victim of the waywardness of male passion—in the Baron de la Motte-Fouqué's popular and influential *Undine* (1811). Throughout the nineteenth century the motif was to remain problematic, encouraging writers to strike dozens of new—and sometimes very uncomfortable—poses in the hope of getting a clearer and more controllable view of it.

* * * * * * *

Of all the Romantics, the one most fervently fascinated by the idea of the *femme fatale* was Théophile Gautier, who wrote a whole series of stories in which idealistic young men are beguiled by supernatural lovers. The stories explore a whole spectrum of possible attitudes and evaluations, ranging from the light comedy of "Omphale" (1834) through the feverish melodrama of "La Morte amoureuse" (1836, translated as "Clarimonde"), and the piquant tragedy of "Arria Marcella" (1852) to the wholeheartedly sentimental *Spirite* (1866). Gautier undertook a much more elaborate and much more self-indulgent exploration of sexuality in *Mademoiselle de Maupin* (1835), where the *femme fatale* motif is deployed in a broader context, but his most intensely-focused and lushly stylish *femme fatale* story is the non-supernatural "Une Nuit de Cléopâtre" (1838, translated as "One of Cleopatra's Nights"), which introduces an element of masochism into the grand passion far more striking than that in "Clarimonde," whose hero is not altogether delighted to be rescued from his vampire lover.

The calculated and luxurious exoticism of Gautier's *femmes fatales* is frequently echoed in French literature, and sometimes—as for instance in the work of Gérard de Nerval—vividly amplified. It is hardly surprising, given the delicious notoriety of the (forbidden) works of the so-called Divine Marquis, that their incipient sadistic streak should also be echoed and similarly magnified. Charles Baudelaire, the forefather of the Decadents, was perfectly fascinated by exotic *femmes fatales*, and wrote numerous hymns of praise of them, most notably "Les Métamorphoses du vampire."

Partly in consequence of this chain of influential exemplars, French literature in the latter half of the century is quite saturated by *femmes fatales*. The motif is displayed with particular extravagance in a remarkable series of highly-colored historical romances: Gustave Flaubert's *Salammbô* (1862), Anatole France's *Thaïs* (1890), Pierre Louÿs's *Aphrodite* (1896), and Alfred Jarry's *Messaline* (1900). It also features to notable effect in cynical exercises in misogyny like Barbey D'Aurevilly's *Les Diaboliques* (1874, translated as *The She-Devils*) and Villiers de l'Isle-Adam's *L'Ève Future* (1890, translated as *The Future Eve*), and in conscientiously Decadent works like Rémy de Gourmont's *Lilith* (1892), Rachilde's *La Marquise de Sade* (1887), and Octave Mirbeau's *Le Jardin de supplices* (1899, translated as *Torture Garden*). The most obsessive painter of *femmes fatales*, Gustave Moreau, belonged to the same cultural milieu, and we can also see the power of the motif in less likely places, notably *La Sorcière* (1862, translated as *Satanism and Witchcraft*) by Jules Michelet, a remarkable exercise in historical apologetics which sets out to redeem the supposedly worthy tradition of female magic from the allegedly slanderous abuse heaped upon it by Religion and Science. Many of the notable deployments of the *femme fatale* motif outside France can also be attributed to the specific influence of French writers and fashions. The most obvious example is the early, conscientiously Decadent, work of the Italian writer Gabriele D'Annunzio, especially *Il trionfo della morte* (1894, translated as *The Triumph of Death*); another is provided by Frank Wedekind, a German writer raised in Switzerland, in *Der Erdgeist* (1895, translated as *Earth-Spirit*) and its sequel *Die Büsche der Pandora* (1904, translated as *Pandora's Box*)

The reasons for this astonishing profusion of images are complex. France was a Catholic country, where the propriety of seeking redemption by confessing one's sins was acknowledged, and where a salacious appetite for especially lurid and horrific confessions had been cultivated and lavishly fed for hundreds of years, since the days of Gilles de Rais and Urbain Grandier. France was also the birthplace of Jean-Jacques Rousseau, who had laid down a stern challenge to official morality in proclaiming the virtue of natural affections and the tyrannical perversity of cultural regulation. It was Rousseau who became the philosophical guiding light of French Romanticism and the petty Satan of the Decadents, provoking a war of ideas between adherents of Nature and Artifice in which literary investigations of the role of female glamour in provoking male arousal became a curious battleground. On a less elevated plane, it is also worth noting that syphilis was rife in nineteenth-century Paris, and that several of the notable writers who were fascinated by the fatal consequences of seduction had contracted it. Other European capitals undoubtedly had their fair share of poxy whores, but were much more inclined to deny steadfastly that decent people ever associated with them. France was the most liberal of nineteenth-century nations in terms of what could be publicly admitted, and hence in terms of what writers could produce without worrying overmuch about censorship. In Britain, Germany, and America—all of which produced memorable images of the *femme fatale* during the heyday of Romanticism, further developments were somewhat inhibited, or forced into eccentricity in order to avoid collision with moral strictures.

* * * * * * *

In English fiction, the supernatural *femme fatale* is far more often deployed as a straightforward figure of menace. She is a lesbian vampire in "Carmilla" (1872), a daughter of Pan in "The Great God Pan" (1890) by Arthur Machen, a hagwife with occult powers of attraction in Arthur Conan Doyle's *The Parasite* (1894), an ice-cool shapeshifter in Clemence Housman's *The Were-Wolf* (1896)—and all of these stories end with her destruction, so that the course of ordinary life can be resumed with a deep sigh of relief. Two of the very best English ghost stories are studies of men driven horribly mad by demanding and indestructible visitors from beyond the grave: "How Love Came to Professor Guildea" (1900) by Robert Hichens and "The Beckoning Fair One" (1911) by Oliver Onions.

English stories which take a more tolerant and understanding view of the attraction which the male characters feel when faced by supernatural temptresses often compensate by making their *femme fatales* sociopathically amoral— a pattern found in *Marahuna* (1888) by H. C. Marriott-Watsdon, *The Witch of Prague* (1891) by F. Marion Crawford, and *The Sea Lady* (1902) by H. G. Wells. George MacDonald's attempt to get to grips with the archetypal Christian *femme fatale* myth, *Lilith* (1895), is far too coy

141

about sex to accomplish much, and dissolves into confusion, while W. H. Hudson's *Green Mansions* (1904), which is quite exceptional in its exaggeratedly sentimental and sympathetic portrayal of the nature-spirit Rima, over-humanizes her to the extent of equipping her with moral views which enable the author to avoid coming to terms with her sexuality.

The most sustained and respectful celebration by an English prose writer of the attractive and destructive power of the *femme fatale* is to be found, ironically enough, in the work of the lesbian Vernon Lee, in "Amour Dure" and "Dionea" from *Hauntings* (1890), and "Prince Alberic and the Snake Lady" in *Pope Jacynth and Other Fantastic Tales* (1904). England also produced the first great homosexual fantasy in which the *femme fatale* role is played by a young male: *The Picture of Dorian Gray* (1891) by Oscar Wilde, but both writers were forced into exile. Poets, however, were granted greater licence, and a wholehearted and emotionally feverish adoration of the *femme fatale* is elaborately displayed in the nakedly masochistic works of Algernon Swinburne, especially "Dolores" and "Faustine" (both 1866). Dante Gabriel Rossetti's most memorable *femmes fatales* are to be found in his paintings, but they crop up occasionally in his poems too, notably in "Sister Helen" (1870). A more satirical view of the *femme fatale*, sometimes verging on black comedy, can be found in Arthur O'Shaughnessy's *An Epic of Women* (1870).

Far more in tune with the English temper was the uneasy and awe-stricken contemplation of avid but ultimately impotent female sexuality contained in the work of H. Rider Haggard, particularly in *She* (1887) and its sequels, but also in such works as *The World's Desire* (1890, co-authored with Andrew Lang). *She* was much-imitated, having revealed a formula by which powerful and extraordinarily sexy women could be accommodated within plots which never had to come into conflict with contemporary morality, and there is a certain eccentric propriety in the fact that so many English literary *femmes fatales* were displaced into tiny enclaves where "lost races" survived in the remote corners of vast trackless wildernesses. It is hardly surprising that it was

142

an Englishman who was eventually to produce the most sarcastic *reductio ad absurdum* of the *femme fatale* motif: Max Beerbohm's *Zuleika Dobson* (1911).

* * * * * * *

In America, the early precedents set by Edgar Allan Poe had far less influence than they had in France, where such stories as "Berenice" (1833), "Morella" (1835), and "Ligeia" (1838) were all translated by Baudelaire. The American *femme fatale* was rapidly retired to such studied moral fables as Nathaniel Hawthorne's "Rappaccini's Daughter" (1844) and Oliver Wendell Holmes's *Elsie Venner* (1859), although there is an intriguing supernatural female contemplated from afar (with no hope that the gulf which separates her from her observer could possibly be crossed) in Fitz-James O'Brien's "The Diamond Lens" (1858).

Even by comparison with England, the *femme fatale* is conspicuous by her absence from late nineteenth-century American fiction. It is also notable that when pulp fiction writers in the early years of the twentieth century began to send heroic adventurers into imaginary worlds far more peculiar than any imagined before, the women they met there—however exotically glamorous they might be—showed a remarkable willingness to become submissive wives. It mattered not whether they were egg-laying Martian princesses, as in Edgar Rice Burroughs's *A Princess of Mars* (1912), or inhabitants of an atomic microcosm, as in Ray Cummings's "The Girl in the Golden Atom" (1919), or fairy-like creatures with butterfly wings, as in Ralph Milne Farley's *The Radio Man* (1924); the principles of literary respectability demanded that they must fall in love by the book and marry before any serious thought of hanky-panky could be permitted to cross their minds. These stories follow a pattern initially laid down by Robert W. Chambers in "The Maker of Moons" (1896), which represented a decisive step towards careful conventionality by comparison with his much more intense French-influenced timeslip romance "The Demoiselle d'Ys" (1896). Only A. Merritt, author of the most exotic of early pulp magazine odysseys in exotica, dared to allow one of his heroes briefly to lament the fact that he had ended up with the nice girl instead of the far sexier witch-woman who had been her rival, and that was not until 1932, in *Dwellers in the Mirage*.

This situation was sufficiently absurd to attract the attention of several notable satirists, who provided scathingly sarcastic commentaries on the prudish refusal of American fiction to acknowledge female sexuality or the potential sexiness of fabulous females. The most notable of these satirists was James Branch Cabell, who mocked American attitudes to sex in a series of flirtatious comedies beginning with *The Cream of the Jest* (1917). This and many works by Cabell offer significant, if sometimes fleeting, glimpses of an idealized exotic female named Ettarre, who is explicitly represented as a paradoxical archetype of male sexual desire, but is never threatening in the way that true *femmes fatales* are. She features most prominently in two melancholy short stories, "The Music from Behind the Moon" (1926) and "The Way of Ecben" (1927). A more slickly cynical kind of satire can be found in the sarcastic allegories of John Erskine, most notably *The Private Life of Helen of Troy* (1925) and *Adam and Eve* (1927), the latter of which exhibits considerable sympathy for Lilith, but maintains its misogynistic credentials by putting the boot into Eve in no uncertain terms. This was to become a favorite tactic of American satirists, who often presented sexy women as misunderstood hedonists whose lack of hypocrisy makes them morally superior to wives. This attitude can be seen in the works of the mildly salacious humorist Thorne Smith, and it is rather ironic that the only real *femme fatale* in his canon was foisted on him by a posthumous collaborator, Norman Matson, in *The Passionate Witch* (1941). Even she was to be carefully domesticated in the film version of the story, *I Married a Witch* and the subsequent TV series *Bewitched*, as was the witch in John van Druten's play (also successfully filmed), *Bell, Book, and Candle* (1951).

American pulp fiction did eventually find room for *femmes fatales* in the pages of the horror story pulp *Weird Tales*, which featured conventionally nasty glamorous female vampires and werewolves in some profusion. *Weird Tales* briefly played host to the one American writer who was significantly and deeply affected by French Romanticism and Decadence, Clark Ashton Smith, whose several *femme fatale* stories include two—"The Witchcraft of Ulua" (1934) and "Mother of Toads" (1937)—which warranted recent re-issue in unexpurgated versions. Curiously enough, it was in the borderlands where pulp weird fiction overlapped the nascent science fiction genre that the *femme fatale* obtained a new lease of life. Science fantasy, as the hybrid genre has sometimes been called, set out to combine the lurid exoticism of Burroughsian interplanetary fantasy with the harder logical edge and more fertile teratological imagination of science fiction. An important early example is C. L. Moore's story of a Martian Medusa, "Shambleau" (1933), and Moore went on to produce other stories in the same vein, including "Black Thirst" (1934), "Julhi" (1935), and "Yvala" (1936). Jack Williamson played science-fictional tricks with time in order that the hero of *The Legion of Time* (1938) could have the *femme fatale* and the nice girl rolled into one, but achieved a more significant subversion of convention in *Darker Than You Think* (1940), in which the hero is given leave to throw in his lot with the lycanthropic sorceress who has beguiled him. Later writers working on this fringe were to produce some of the most interesting modern stories of *femmes fatales*. These include Fritz Leiber's "The Girl With the Hungry Eyes" (1949), Robert F. Young's "To Fell a Tree" (1959), and Theodore Sturgeon's "Bianca's Hands" (1960). Also notable as a writer of science fantasy is the British writer J. G. Ballard, who wrote a number of deftly ironic *femme fatale* stories, including several of the items in his collection *Vermilion Sands* (1971).

* * * * * * *

Although it emerged from rather different nineteenth-century roots, the eventual development of the American situation mirrors the fate of the *femme fatale* in twentieth-century Europe. Once her heyday in *fin de siècle* France was over she became a rather enfeebled creature, thoroughly demystified even though she was never quite completely or convincingly explained by the theories of Freud and his successors. Once the libido was brought into the arena of clinical study it became a chimera of a rather different stripe, and the occult power of the *femme fatale* was reduced to something much more ordinary. She became a mere *cliché*, or—even worse—a figure of fun. She became understandable, a deserving recipient of civilized tolerance more to be pitied than condemned.

The cinema, which gave the *femme fatale* a new visual image in characters memorably played by Theda Bara and Marlene Dietrich, also played a major part in reducing her ruthlessly to merely human dimensions. As in pulp fiction, convention demanded that—in Hollywood, at least—all *femmes fatales* should either accept domestication or die. Even this humiliation was not the end; dissatisfaction with the female stereotypes contained in the media was a significant aspect of the feminist movement, and some of the feminist writers who attempted to redress the cultural balance were prepared to re-appraise the psychological implications of *femme fatale* figures. Their work has provided a new dimension of satirical irony for the subversion and mockery of the motif, which is clearly evident in such novels as Angela Carter's *The Passion of New Eve* (1977).

But this relative decline in the power of the image does not mean that the problematic conflict of ideas which spawned the image has been solved. Sexuality still sings the same old siren song, and the old taboos—albeit weaker and more flexible—are still in place. The discipline of official morality is no longer as strict or severe as it once was, and that softening is reflected in the character of modern *femmes fatales*, who are far more often victims than villains, but as feminists constantly point out and lament, female sexuality has not yet been liberated from its straitjacket, and the demands which men make of their lovers and wives remain paradoxical as well as oppressive. Shifting the blame for infidelity is as popular as it ever was—and just as stupidly dishonest and hypocritical. It is still written into the fine print of the social contract that women cannot win.

While this situation endures, the *femme fatale* can never entirely lose her glamour or her dramatic potential. A shadow of her former self she may be, but there is an undeniable aesthetic appeal in the enigmatic character of shadows. The modern *femme fatale* story is inevitably more analytical and more subtly ironic than its nineteenth-century ancestors; it is often apologetically urbane or flippantly witty—and yet it cannot entirely hide or set aside the anxiety which underlies it. And we must remember that the conquest of venereal disease by antibiotics has proved in the end to be temporary; the whores who function as an extra-marital outlet for the more exotic desires of so many men are once again becoming carriers of a sinister plague. The story is not over; a new chapter has already begun.

XI.

WHAT WE KNOW ABOUT VAMPIRES

The folkloristic origins of vampire mythology are described at some length in Paul Barber's scholarly treatise on *Vampires, Burial and Death: Folklore and Reality* (1988), which attempts to breathe a cold wind of reason through the fevered mass of legends and rumors collected by earlier writers like Montague Summers. Barber's thesis, put in a nutshell, is that the attributes of the folkloric vampire are mostly derived from observations of what happens to corpses as they decay. He belongs to a species of sceptic who might be called rationalizers: people who attempt to subvert reports of supernatural phenomena by arguing that what actually occurred was a natural phenomenon which was misinterpreted by virtue of the ignorance of the observers and/or the stressful circumstances in which the observation was made.

There is undoubtedly a certain measure of enlightenment to be gained by Barber's philosophical method, and when he deals with "actual" vampire panics of the kind on which he understandably chooses to focus his claims to have "explained" them are reasonably well-grounded. There are, however, other aspects of the mythology to which he gives less attention. He has, perforce, to dedicate several chapters of his work to less substantial revenants: ghostly shades whose reappearance is indeed only apparent, and has to be explained in psychological terms as a subjective experience involving memory, guilt and the power of the imagination. In these chapters his rationalisations refer to mistakes of a rather different kind.

Even the expanded version of Barber's argument does not, however, suffice to account for the whole spectrum of vampire mythology. What is more, it is at least arguable that the residue he leaves virtually untouched is in fact the most interesting part of vampire folklore. It is, at any rate, the part whose influence is most evident in the vampire fiction of the last two centuries.

* * * * * * *

Insofar as creators of literary vampires have relied on information about "real" vampires the primal source of what they "knew"—often at second or third hand—was a treatise on vampires compiled by a Roman Catholic clergyman named Dom Augustine Calmet in the mid-eighteenth century. This was published (as part of a longer work) in Paris in 1746 and in London in 1759 and was reprinted several times thereafter, reappearing in 19th century Britain as part of *The Phantom World*.

Sensationally-inclined books on occult subjects were very popular in the eighteenth century, although they flew in the face of strident claims that an Age of Enlightenment had been attained and a final victory over superstition. Calmet's thesis arrived in a London which had already thrilled to multiple editions of Daniel Defoe's *History of the Devil* (1726) and *A System of Magic* (1727), and would still be ready a century later to marvel at Walter Scott's *Letters on Demonology and Witchcraft* (1830). Its revelations filtered into a kind of cultural undergrowth which only had to bide its time until the explosive pressure of modern cultivation turned it into a veritable jungle.

Much of the material in Calmet's compendium is of the kind which Barber discusses at length, but the excerpts which Christopher Frayling selects for reprinting in *Vampyres: Lord Byron to Count Dracula* (1991) begin with a very deferent "case." The story in question is reproduced from a book by Philostratus chronicling the exploits of the legendary magician Apollonius of Tyana, although it is there attributed to one Phlegon of Tralles. Its elements echo far more resonantly in the literary tradition which is Frayling's main focus than anything explicable in Barber's terms. It tells of a female revenant who visits her "gallant" night after night, apparently receiving a warm welcome.

There is no reference to blood-drinking in Phlegon's account but many readers and hearers of the tale obviously found it easy to link the returning lover to the mythical lamias: demons sent forth by Hecate in the guise of beautiful girls to seduce and prey upon young men. Frayling's excerpt concludes with Calmet's oblique but highly significant comment on the case: "We know what illicit love is capable of, and how far it may lead anyone who is devoured by a violent passion...."[1]

Here is the heart and soul of the modern vampire mythology which has been forged by literateurs. Modern vampires are not rotting corpses whose decay-induced appearances of continued activity have been mistaken for signs of life, nor are they mere shades summoned by wayward memory or lingering guilt; they are the products of that kind of violent passion which leads to "illicit love."

Frayling also calls attention to another account of a lamia contained in Philostratus's life of Apollonius of Tyana, which had been reproduced in Robert Burton's *Anatomy of Melancholy* (1621) and was thus well-known to writers associated with the English Romantic movement—it is the basis of a famous poem by Keats. Frayling's history of vampires explains how lamiaesque female vampires obtained male counterparts modelled on Lord Byron and hence gave eventual birth to the modern archetype of Count Dracula. Thus did vampirism become a kind of "illicit love" available to both sexes, necessarily involving "violent passions."

It is, however, not the substance of Calmet's judgment that I want to address here but its curious introduction. What on earth can Calmet mean by the first two words of that vital sentence reproduced by Frayling? What is it that he thinks we know about the capabilities of illicit love, and how do we come to know it? If we are to understand the awesome power of the vampire myth and the astonishing popularity which the motif has lately come to enjoy—not merely in literary fantasy but in lifestyle fantasy too—we must ask how it comes to be the case that the idea of sexy revenants seducing us in order to suck the blood from our bodies somehow seems utterly reasonable to us. If we are to understand the fascination which the vampire exerts upon us, we must ask ourselves what it is that we already know about love and passion—without, perhaps, quite being able to articulate it— which facilitates our response to its seductive advances.

* * * * * * *

We can, of course, only speculate as to the precise details of what Dom Augustine Calmet knew about "what illicit love is capable of." Had he desired to tell us—which he almost certainly did not—he would not have been able to do it, for any such reportage would have been considered unprintable. We can, however, be reasonably sure that he was not speaking merely as an interpreter of the scriptures. If we had to rely on the Bible for an account of "what illicit love is capable of" we would be forever compelled to languish in ignorance—although we would, of course, obtain a fairly good idea of what those who disapprove of "illicit love" are capable of. (See, for instance, Numbers 25, where Phineas—at Moses's behest—impales two young lovers with a single thrust of his spear because the girl in question happens to be a Midianite, and hence not fit company for an Israelite.)

Although we have no idea what Calmet's own sexual preferences were, we can nevertheless be reasonably sure of one thing, and that is that his faith urged him to suppress them. Whether he succeeded in doing so or not, charity requires us to suppose that he must have tried. This supposition has certain corollaries.

The perennial problem faced by Catholic clergymen who attempt to repress their sexual impulses is that they are fighting against physiology. It is, according to medical rumor, not impossible to win the battle of mind over matter, to the extent that production of semen actually stops, but even when victory is won it must be hard-fought. While the fight goes on (and the probability is that for the majority it goes on indefinitely) the semen has to be disposed of somehow. Given that masturbation and fornication are both deemed to be sinful, the conscientious clergyman is highly likely to experience erotic dreams and "nocturnal emissions"—and even then is likely to feel acute pangs of conscience.

The Catholic Church may have ways of coping with this problem which are moderately successful, but as laymen have no idea what goes on between priests in the privacy of the confessional we can only guess as to the frequency with which sufferers are simply told not to worry about it. There are on record, however, methods of coping which are not so sensible, and these include myths which construe erotic dreams as demonic visitations and a nocturnal emission as a devious act of theft by a "succubus." The succubus is, in effect, a Christian version of the lamia: a seductress sent by some malevolent higher power, which lies in wait for young men with predatory intent.

Even in the medically well-informed world of today it is not unusual for common parlance to lump blood and semen together under the heading of "vital fluids." Indeed, the recent advent of AIDS has lent an ironic and macabre cutting edge to such conflationary euphemisms as "the exchange of bodily fluids." In the past, of course, the combination of ideas was unavoidable. The idea that the essential "force" of life was bound up with blood and semen was difficult to avoid in a world which thought of health and emotion as products of the flux and disturbance of "bodily humours." The link between female sexuality and blood is, of course, more obvious, not merely by virtue of the phenomenon of menstruation and its association with female sexual maturity, but also in respect of the bloodshed traditionally associated with a female's loss of virginity.

In France, the word sang, whose literal reference is to blood, used to be one of the euphemisms employed to refer to semen. A notable vampire story which is explicitly developed about that double meaning, with particular reference to female "defloration," is Rémy de Gourmont's "Le Magnolia" (c. 1890). The pun is inevitably lost in the translation included in the Gourmont collection *The Angels of Perversity* (1992), but the symbolism of the story remains very striking. This is one of the earliest stories to refer to the double puncture-mark which has since become an iconic stigma of vampiric attack (in spite of the inconceivability of any such mark being inflicted by human canine teeth, however extended).

Although the physiological pressure of semen-generation is unique to the male sex, women are by no means immune to psychological pressures of a sexual nature. The nuns of Dom Augustine Calmet's day, like the priests, were commanded to repress such feelings, and when those desires surfaced in dreams they too could easily be regarded by the anxiously conscience-stricken as demonic visitations. One of the most celebrated of all sorcery trials—that of Urbain Grandier in 1633-34, which was dramatized by Aldous Huxley in *The Devils of Loudun* (1952) and filmed by Ken Russell as *The Devils* (1971)—involved the accusation that a notoriously uncelibate priest had afflicted the superior of a convent and many of her charges with demons of lust. Thus was the mythology of the succubus extended to include the incubus, just as the myth of the vampiric lamia was extended to include a male counterpart.

In view of all this, we can be reasonably confident in declaring that a very significant part of what Dom Augustine Calmet knew about the capabilities of illicit love and the avidity of violent passion was that even the most pious man's dreams were apt to be troubled by mysterious and irresistible visitors, whose temptations were dangerously apt to leave an embarrassingly evident stain. This helps us to understand why he was able to read Phlegon's story (the original of which contains no reference to blood-drinking) in such a way as to transmute it into a vampire story of unusual potency—and perhaps why he then went on to bury it in an untidy heap of materials that were far less disturbing. It also helps us to understand why his attempt to hide the tree in the forest failed. There is a certain delicious inevitability about the way that vampires analogous to succubi and incubi were eventually able to emerge from their temporary interment, not as hideous ghouls or pathetic shades but as handsome creatures possessed of a magisterial grandeur, as if they were gorgeous butterflies bursting forth from shabby cocoons.

* * * * * * *

The optimists of the Enlightenment assumed that the popularity of such superstitious works as Calmet's would decline. They assumed that the continued sophistication of scientific knowledge and the continued spread of literacy and education would put an end to all such follies of the vulgar mind. In fact, the reverse was the case. The spread of literacy and education to the masses permitted and facilitated an extraordinary proliferation and diversification of alternatives to the orthodox wisdom of the cultural *élite*. Not only did the popular superstitions of the eighteenth century survive and thrive but many similar ideas which had fallen from fashionability gained new leases of life, and new notions of a similar kind were invented on a massive scale.

The optimists of the Enlightenment also thought that crime and social dissent would decrease as the increasing wealth of society allowed the fundamental needs of the majority of men to be better met. In fact, the enrichment of society, far from decreasing the dissatisfactions reflected in all kinds of "deviant behaviour," magnified and encouraged them. The same kind of seemingly-paradoxical pattern is, of course, reflected in the private arena of inner life, most particularly of all in the important part of that life which is concerned with sexual feeling and activity.

Nowadays we know far more about blood and semen than was known in Dom Augustine Calmet's day. We understand the mechanism of nocturnal emission; we know that erotic dreams are not the sendings of malevolent demons intent on obtaining our damnation; we can decode and analyse all kinds of sexual symbolism. Thanks to Dr. Kinsey, agony columns, Masters and Johnson, *Playboy*, Shere Hite, and *The News of the World* we really do know—far better, at any rate, than Dom Augustine Calmet did—what "illicit love" is actually capable of, and to what extremes people "devoured" by violent passion may be led.

Unfortunately, the fact that we know such things as these often serves to amplify rather than to dispel our confusion. To take a trivial example, we live in a world where we are bombarded day in and day out by advertisements for washing powder which go to extraordinary lengths to inform us that we really needn't worry any more about such obscenely stubborn stains as those caused by "blackcurrant juice" because some magical "biological" ingredient is absolutely guaranteed to dissolve and eradicate them. Knowing that the message the advertiser is trying to get across is that this brand will get blood-stains out of your knickers doesn't make it any easier to say—but the fact that advertisers make such extravagantly strenuous efforts, and that their activity serves to maintain fierce competition between a dozen effectively-identical products, is eloquent testimony to the levels of anxiety involved.

There has grown up in the modern world a body of information about human sexuality which would be mountainous even if one could sort out and remove from it the masses of misinformation (unfortunate errors) and disinformation (downright lies) which still vexatiously pollute it. It is dubious whether even the self-supposed experts who claim to have scaled the heights of the mountain have really taken its lessons to heart, or gained much personal benefit therefrom, but one thing that is certain is that it looms over entrants into the novitiate of puberty like the north face of the Eiger over a one-armed asthmatic in ballet shoes.

Given this, it is not so very difficult to understand why the incubus/succubus kind of vampire has never been conclusively staked through the heart and put away. Nor is it so very strange that he/she has become instead a suspiciously equivocal emblem of freedom and release.

Dom Augustine Calmet's vow of chastity might have put him in a difficult situation, but at least it was a simple situation; the lines confining him were clearly drawn. Any temptation which threatened to draw him across those lines was automatically categorized as the kind of thing from which a good man must avert his eyes, while raising up the protective power of the Holy Cross. Nowadays, we are properly grateful for the fact that many of the strictures constraining expression of our sexuality have been removed, and that many of the boundaries channeling that expression have been relaxed. Alas, where possibilities multiply, stresses and strains may still increase, especially when so many of the possibilities that are no-longer-forbidden still carry a fear-some burden of sharp anxiety and secret shame.

Nowadays, one is likely not only to feel guilty about whatever sexual impulses one happens to feel, but also to feel guilty about feeling guilty (and so on). There is, of course, no way out of this recursive maze in the real world, nor even in the world of the imagination insofar as it is restricted to grappling with actual possibilities. In such desperate circumstances, the frankly fantastic images which supplied the demons of yesterday may now supply saviors of a sort. By definition, vampires are unbound by the limits of human knowledge and free from the mediocrity of actual human capability—and their need-driven impulses, however perverse (in every sense of the word) they might seem, are refreshingly straightforward.

Nobody with an atom of sense or feeling could possibly want to take the place of an ignorant novice such as Dom Augustine Calmet must once have been before he turned his hand to scholarship, with no viable effective instrument to solve the puzzling contradiction of lurid dreams and holy vows. If, however, one could forget about the holy vows while retaining the full force of the lurid dreams, and bring to bear upon their substance a psychological device which would make them more pleasurable still, that would be a different matter. Nocturnal tempters are no trouble at all if one may embrace them gladly, and indulge them freely and wholeheartedly—and if one can take the further imaginative step which leads one into the dreamworld from which such tempters come, not merely entertaining them but becoming one with them, why should anyone refuse? Dreams are, after all, merely dreams.

* * * * * * *

What we know about vampires now is that they are neither rotting corpses impossibly returned from their graves nor intangible phantoms glimpsed in a dim light and therefore misidentified. They are, instead, clearly-seen and sharply-defined visions which, although they cannot hurt us, really can grip us. We know that they grip us in an authentically visceral fashion, and we know that the experience has far more pleasure than pain in it. The ability to indulge such knowledge in the privacy of inner space—which is, of course, the only space in which such things as vampires can exist—is a gift for which we ought to be thankful, and in respect of which we need not entertain the least vestige of shame or anxiety.

XII.

A BRIEF HISTORY OF VAMPIRES

Folkloristic vampires are of several different kinds, depending on their cultural origins, but only two kinds are of much relevance to the development of modern literary vampires and contemporary vampire imagery. The older of the two, in terms of pertinent records, is the Greek lamia. Lamias were a subcategory of empusas, which were monstrous phantoms sent by the goddess Hecate to frighten or devour human beings (usually travellers); lamias had the particular trick of assuming the form of beautiful women in order to waylay young men and suck their blood. Some accounts claimed that the lamia's natural form was serpentine.

The lamia, who was popularized on a modest scale by Classical scholars, was able to make her way into literary fiction without significant modification, her story-value being obvious from the outset. Such figures are sometimes echoed in later folk tales of "fairy brides," although the brides in question are often innocent of any malice, as in the famous tale of Melusine, who periodically changed into a snake. John Keats's poem "Lamia" (1820) is based on a Classical tale by Philostratus but echoes the story of Melusine in taking a sympathetic view of its central character.

A menacing lamia-like vampire is featured in a story variously called "Wake Not the Dead!" and "The Bride of the Grave," which first appeared in English in the 1820s, falsely attributed to the German writer Ludwig Tieck. By far the most striking nineteenth-century image of this kind is Théophile Gautier's "La Morte amoureuse" (1836), usually translated as "Clarimonde." Although Gautier, like Keats, has his young hero "saved" by the intervention of an older and wiser man he remains rather ambivalent as to whether the young man might not have been immeasurably better off had he not been forced to abandon his parasitic lover, even though he would certainly have died. In his later and very similar "Arria Marcella" (1852), Gautier was prepared to state forthrightly that its young hero could never contemplate a relationship with any merely human woman after having known the eponymous phantom courtesan.

The second, and far more common, kind of literary vampire is associated with Eastern Europe—particularly, of course, with Transylvania. As Paul Barber explains in his excellent book, *Vampires, Burial, and Death: Folklore and Reality* (1988), however, the vampire of Eastern European folklore bears very little resemblance to the literary vampire who notionally owes his origins to the legends of that region.

The vampire of Eastern European folklore is essentially an animated corpse, which manifests a whole range of deeply unpleasant symptoms and behaviors exaggerating and extrapolating the kinds of changes which corpses actually undergo as they decay. It is this kind of vampire which sparked off a tradition of scholarly fantasy in the early eighteenth century, when Austrian forces occupied Serbia and Wallachia and began sending back reports of unusual funerary practises, whose purpose was to ensure that corpses remained in their graves rather than returning to prey upon the living. Such reports were discussed in a now-celebrated essay by a French churchman named Dom Augustine Calmet, which formed a chapter of his *Dissertations sur les apparitions des anges, des démons et des esprits* (1746, translated as *The Phantom World*, 1850).

In planning *Dracula* (1897) Bram Stoker borrowed certain details from this folkloristic tradition, having first heard about it from a Hungarian academic named Arminius Vambery when Vambery was a guest at the Beefsteak Club (which Stoker ran on behalf of his employer, the actor Henry Irving). He consulted Calmet too, but he also had two earlier literary works very much in mind, which caused him considerably to modify the material he found there. His own story was partly inspired by a desire to emulate J. Sheridan Le

Fanu's famous novelette "Carmilla" (1872)—Stoker and Le Fanu had both attended Trinity College, Dublin, and Le Fanu was editor of the *Dublin University Magazine* when Stoker submitted his earliest stories to it. "Carmilla" transplants a lamia-like vampire into an alien geographical context not so very far from the one Stoker used.

Stoker also borrowed inspiration from John Polidori's *The Vampyre* (1819), a bizarre hymn of hate directed against Lord Byron, who is caricatured in the story as Lord Ruthven—a name borrowed from the villain of Lady Caroline Lamb's *Glenarvon* (1816), which was an equally embittered fictionalization of Lady Caroline's love affair with the man she characterized as "mad, bad and dangerous to know." Polidori had been Byron's doctor and confidant for a while and seems to have been eaten up by envy of him; what Stoker secretly thought of his own highly charismatic and aristocratic employer we can only guess, but he went back to Arminius Vambery in search of an aristocratic model for the "king-vampire" who had figured in one of his nightmares. Vambery suggested the fifteenth-century Voivode Vlad Tepes, "the Impaler," whose family name was Dragul (Dracul in the Latinized version), but whose scribes usually signed him Dragulya, meaning "son of Dragul," to distinguish him from his similarly-named father. In spite of his reputation for cruelty—widely advertised and probably much exaggerated by one Michael Beheim, who carried news of his exploits into Western Europe—Vlad Tepes was (and is) regarded as a great hero in his own land, which he liberated from the oppressive occupation of the Turks.

The runaway success of Stoker's *Dracula* (1897) was not in itself sufficient to secure the image of the male vampire as a handsome aristocrat requiring relatively little in the way of supernatural aid to be supremely attractive to women. The first (pirated) film version of the novel, Friedrich Murnau's *Nosferatu* (1922), cast Max Schreck as a hideously monstrous "Graf von Orlok," but Tod Browning's 1930 version with Bela Lugosi as Dracula provided the definitive visual image of which almost all subsequent cinematic and literary versions have been copies. Montague Summers's classic scholarly fantasy *The Vampire: His Kith and Kin* (1928)

161

came far to late to rescue the "true" vampire from the symbolic transformations which had by then overtaken the notion.

* * * * * * *

Stoker's *Dracula* is supposed to be an incarnation of pure evil, but this role is slightly confused even in the original text. In the dream which provided the seed from which the story grew the "king-vampire" appeared only at the end, interrupting the female vampires who posed a more immediate threat to the dreamer—as they do, in the text, to Jonathan Harker. In the melodramatic chapter deleted from the novel and separately published as "Dracula's Guest," Dracula is again responsible (seemingly, at least) for saving Harker from an urgent threat. The main threat which he subsequently poses is that of conferring extraordinary sexual attractiveness and a kind of immortality on the novel's two main female characters, Lucy and Mina—a fate which Stoker declared to be far worse than death but which had already been viewed in a rather different light in the work of Keats, Gautier, and others.

While Victoria was on the English throne all overt mention of sexual matters in fiction was considered indecent, but it was possible in those pre-Freudian times for vividly erotic passages to be presented in symbolic disguises which seem quite transparent to the modern reader. Marie Corelli, the best-selling writer of Stoker's day, disguised her vivid accounts of erotic arousal with pious religious terminology but the language of demonic possession was more powerful and perhaps more accurately reflective of the moral anxiety in which all sexual experience was (and, to some extent, still is) shrouded.

"Carmilla" and *Dracula* are among the most strikingly erotic works published in the Victorian era, and one cannot help suspecting that their conscientiously strident representation of sexual attraction as a manifest evil is either blatantly neurotic or a trifle hypocritical. French fiction of the period—especially that associated with the Decadent Movement—is much more explicit with respect to the sexual nature of vampirism; Rémy de Gourmont's symbolist fantasy "Le Magnolia" (1895, translated as "The Magnolia") uses the word sang to signify semen as well as blood, while Jean Lorrain's "Le Verre de sang" (1893, translated as "The Glass of Blood") is a tale of lesbian paedophilia in which the junior partner is afflicted with a wasting disease whose medical treatment involves drinking fresh blood. The opium-dream sequence in Lorrain's *Monsieur de Phocas* (1900, translated 1993) also links vampirism to lesbianism.

The aggressive rigidity of declared Victorian morality relaxed after the turn of the century, but the censorship associated with it persisted. By the time that censorship was sufficiently weakened to be broken a considerable burden of frustration and resentment had built up behind it. It was perhaps inevitable that when the literary and cinematic images of the vampire became fully available for profound and drastic reassessment the opportunity would be seized with relish.

The American cinema was subject to rigorous censorship in the period in which Browning's *Dracula* was made. Overt displays of sexual activity were strictly taboo, and any interference with the "natural" course of sexual attraction had to be ritually demonized. The symbolism of vampire stories could hardly be ignored now—whether Freud's theories were true or not they had been very widely popularized and had taken firm root in the imagination—and vampire films had to be far more careful in their covert implications than Stoker's text. One effect of this awareness was the importation into the cinematic image of a note of dark irony—a reaction which fits in perfectly with Freud's theory of humor. Lugosi's most famous lines ("Children of the night—what music they make!" and "I never drink...wine") lend a nudging slyness to his entire performance—an element of wit which only required mild exaggeration to be subsequently converted into pure comedy in such excessively-knowing films as *Love at First Bite* (1979).

* * * * * * *

Once the censorship which held sway in Britain and America until the late 1950s went into a rapid decline, the

163

vampire became available for use in stories which challenged and overturned the assumptions encoded in the figure of Dracula. Writers reacting against the demonization of sexual feeling began to look at the vampire in a new way. In Theodore Sturgeon's *Some of Your Blood* (1961) a vampire finds a logical and harmless private solution to his problematic compulsion, but cannot contend with the horror this arouses in the larger society. In Jane Gaskell's *The Shiny Narrow Grin* (1964), however, a teenage girl who is a typical product of her era finds nothing particularly terrible in the prospect of a romance with a vampire—a prospect made doubly attractive by the innate glamour of the notion and the potential such a liaison has as evidence of liberation from the moral values of the older generation.

In films, of course, censorship clung on more determinedly. The Hammer horror films which gave Dracula a new lease of life, most notably in his personification by Christopher Lee, were always careful to end with a triumph of "good"—often symbolized by a suspiciously makeshift cross—over "evil." The sheer profusion of the films ensured, however, that every conclusion of this sort had to be perceived as a mere holding action, a Canute-like gesture in the face of an inevitable tide. Few people could ever have been in doubt that the gratifications obtained by their audiences were gleaned from the films' elaborate foreplay, not their knee-jerk climaxes.

The Hammer films and their imitations usually retained the elaborate system of rules which Stoker had devised for the conduct and control of vampires: their vulnerability to stakes through the heart, fire, and daylight; their allergy to garlic and key symbols of the Christian mythos; their difficulties with running water and the failure of mirrors to reflect their images. These were equally useful in facilitating hairbreadth escapes and orchestrating conclusions. Writers who wanted to place the vampire in a more "realistic" and morally neutral context inevitably found some of these rules too absurd to be entertained, and others inconveniently restrictive. There rapidly grew up in the mid-1970s a school of "revisionist" vampire fiction which dispensed with selected components of this characterisation on an ad hoc basis.

Some such stories abandoned even the fundamental notion that the vampire was a revenant returned from the dead and substituted a different human species—perhaps one of a whole series of such species—living secretly among us. This greatly facilitated the moral re-evaluation of the vampire, in allowing the argument that there might be no reason why a member of a different species, which preys on humans by virtue of its intrinsic nature, should have any more moral consideration for its victims than we have for cattle. Stories of this kind include Suzy McKee Charnas's *The Vampire Tapestry* (1980), Nancy Collins's *Sunglasses After Dark* (1989), and Poppy Z. Brite's *Lost Souls* (1992). To date, however, by far the most successful of the revisionist vampire stories have been those which retain as much of the Stokeresque stereotype as reason and ingenuity will permit. Anne Rice's series begun with *Interview with the Vampire* (1976) reached international best-seller status. Chelsea Quinn Yarbro's series featuring the Comte St. Germain, begun with *Hôtel Transylvania* (1978), belong to the same subcategory. Fred Saberhagen's *The Dracula Tape* (1975), which carefully and convincingly reinterprets the substance of Stoker's text so that Dracula becomes a misunderstood altruist while Van Helsing is a holy fool, offers both the clearest and most slyly ironic example of how Victorian anxiety might be converted into enlightened admiration. The complex romantic appeal of the Byronic vampire is celebrated and intelligently analysed by numerous lushly erotic novels, including Freda Warrington's *A Taste of Blood Wine* (1992).

The one element of the original characterisation which is very insistently abandoned by all these stories is the vulnerability of the vampire to the symbols of Christian religion. In making much of this matter the writers affiliate their work to a rich tradition of "literary Satanism," which constructs apologias for Christian representations of evil as a means of questioning the narrow and perhaps misconceived definition of "good" which the Church has traditionally sought to impose. Anne Rice's stories generally take the form of difficult but worthwhile existential odysseys from fearful superstition and self-hatred to liberating and increasingly bold freethought. Yarbro's *The Palace* (1979) contains a scathing attack on the fundamentalist ideology, here embodied in the character of Savonarola. As might be expected, this line of argument is more spectacularly displayed in French fiction, most notably in Pierre Kast's stridently anticlerical and vividly erotic *The Vampires of Alfama* (1975, translated 1976).

* * * * * * *

Anne Rice's elaborate exercises in vampire existentialism were intended by their author to be purely hypothetical, but they provided a philosophical foundation for lifestyle fantasy which had not existed before. Lifestyle fantasies echoing the the values of literary Satanism had long embraced witchcraft, paganism and various other kinds of occultism but had rarely borrowed anything from vampire mythology (although the most flamboyantly eccentric contributor to the short-lived English Decadent Movement of the early 1890s, Count Stenbock, put it about that he liked to sleep in a coffin).

The generation of teenagers whose attitudes were celebrated by Jane Gaskell was followed some 10-20 years later by a generation whose declared alienation was far more extreme, made manifest in the stylistic extremes of the punk subculture. One subspecies of punk, initially categorized by journalists as "Gothic punk," took its stylistic cues from Siouxsie of Siouxsie and the Banshees and Robert Smith of The Cure, favoring dyed-black hair, all-black apparel (ameliorated by silver jewellery and the occasional hint of red velvet) and vividly exotic eye make-up. As the punk era withered away, the Goths remained, forming a more persistent subculture which rapidly evolved to take aboard a more abundant imagery, including much imagery associated with vampirism. Some of the bands favored by this subculture, including The Damned and The Sisters of Mercy, cultivated a mock-sinister appearance and shadowed performing style without importing much dark fantasy into their lyrics, but the

166

eclectically-inclined Bauhaus borrowed from horror films as well as other sources, and made much of their nine-minute anthem "Bela Lugosi Is Dead." Fields of the Nephilim began to cultivate an earnest mystical paganism which reached its apogee in the brilliant *Elizium* album (1990).

Several bands formed in the late '80s—most notably the UK's Nosferatu, America's The Dream Theatre, Finland's Two Witches, and Germany's typically extreme Sopor Aeternus and the Ensemble of Shadows—linked their appearance, their ideology, and their lyrics specifically to vampire imagery, and vampirism is prolifically and powerfully featured in the work of the pagan band Incubus Succubus (recently renamed Inkubus Sukkubus). Fan organisations associated with this subculture include two versions of The Vampyre Society, The Gothic Society (the publicity arm of the band Nosferatu), and Thee Vampire Guild. The last-named offers two compilation CDs of vampire music called *What Sweet Music They Make*, and two further compilation tapes of Goth music are distributed by the House of Dracula, home of the fanzine *Bats and Red Velvet*. These same organizations provide gathering points for lifestyle fantasists interested in vampirism.

Lifestyle fantasists very rarely represent themselves as actual vampires, this being a much less convenient fantasy than electing actually to be a witch or a celebrant of pagan rites. Their identification is of a more oblique kind, by which they become fellow travellers on an existential journey very similar—in terms of both its values and its troubles—to that undertaken by Anne Rice's protagonists. The most elaborate literary reflection of and homage to this kind of lifestyle fantasy can be found in Poppy Brite's *Lost Souls*, which links teenage angst to vampiric imagery in a brutally uncompromising fashion. As with all occult lifestyle fantasies the practitioners of this philosophy may seem mildly eccentric to outsiders, but they are perfectly entitled to reply that there is not the slightest merit in the determined following of the heavily-advertised and vulgarly commonplace lifestyle fantasies which are the property of the determinedly unimaginative conformist herd. Most such lifestyle fantasists are, of course, wholly conscious of the fact that they are engaged in a fantasy, and might well claim to be less deluded than some more orthodox followers of fashion.

* * * * * * *

The fact that vampirism has become a topic of interest to lifestyle fantasists should not be a surprise, nor should the credit for it be given entirely to the literary exercises in "vampiric existentialism" which provide the philosophical fuel for such identifications. Insofar as it is a visible symptom of adolescent rebellion against the norms of the older generation it will doubtless prove to be a passing fad, because such attempts at gaudy differentiation must be forever in search of novelty, but there is something more profound involved than mere fashion. The revisionist literary fantasies of the last twenty years have a place in a much broader pattern of evolution which reflects a fundamental—and probably irreversible—change in our attitudes.

Stoker's *Dracula* was one of the most lurid and most revealing imaginative products of an era in which "evil" was conceived as something external to the individual and alien to authentic "human nature." Among many other things, the Victorians desperately wanted to believe that the Lucy Westenras and Mina Murrays of this world are innately "pure," innocent of any lustful desires, unless and until something they cannot help and cannot control seizes them in its deadly grip. The very different emphasis of lamia stories serves to remind us that even the most optimistic Victorians found it impossible to maintain this fiction in respect of male sexuality.

The Victorians must have known, of course, that their attitude to female sexuality was a hollow pretence—but that only made them all the more determined in their insistence. Their motives for maintaining this illusion were complicated, but those cynics who suspect that it had much more to do with shoring up the social superiority of the male of the species than deeply-felt convictions about female psychology are surely right.

What Dracula's constant reincarnation and gradual image make-over tell us is, of course, what we really knew all along but were afraid to say clearly: that "evil" is not—and, indeed, cannot be—something external to the individual and alien to authentic human nature, but something within us and intrinsic to our existence. Whatever the vampire symbolizes, he or she can no longer be a supernatural being outside the natural order of things; he or she must instead be something within that natural order: he or she must be an aspect of ourselves. Small wonder, therefore, that we have become interested in exercises in vampiric existentialism, or that we have begun to extend such identifications from literary to participant fantasies. Small wonder, too, that the Byronic male vampire is nowadays a much more straightforward counterpart of the lamia.

We now live in an era in which many people—some of them grudgingly—accept that there is such a thing as female sexuality and that the emotional upheavals which are associated with it need not be demonized as wild and uncontrollable forces in whose grip women are utterly helpless. Much contemporary vampire fiction is concerned with the attempts made by vampires—sometimes young and often female—to take control of their situation and find a way of life which is materially, psychologically, and morally sustainable. They do not always succeed, but even the most blatant fantasy fiction has to maintain a fundamental realism of attitude.

The vampire is especially useful for this kind of self-analysis because—unlike the magisterial magus or the white witch—he or she cannot be entirely sanitized and reduced to harmless puerility. Vampires are essentially predators and parasites; they can be represented as prudent predators or as honest traders who compensate their victims fully for what they take, but take they must and what they take is vitality itself. The use of the lamia or the Byronic vampire as a romantic ideal commits us to recognising a truth which—even in today's supposedly enlightened times—we often find it convenient to ignore: that even the most intimate and loving human relationships involve an element of parasitic exploitation, and that only fools can possibly believe that love is a kind of salvation which requires no further analysis and no further negotiation.

169

XIII.

A BRIEF HISTORY OF WEREWOLVES

The idea that human nature is in some fundamental sense divided is as old as consciousness itself. It is to be found in all kinds of representation: mythical, religious, artistic, and scientific.

Philosophers attempting to analyse the conscious mind very often begin by making some kind of preliminary distinction between the domain of rational control and certain anarchic forces which undermine that domain and continually threaten to smash the tyranny of reason. Plato characterized this enemy within as a complex of "lower appetites" and recommended their ruthless annihilation by the power of the will; most of those who came after him agreed with him. Descartes labelled the subversive passions "animal sprits," while Spinoza, though accepting that emotion must be accepted as an essential part of human nature rather than a defect of it, nevertheless concluded that freedom was based in the rational will and that every victory of the emotions was a kind of enslavement. The implicit politics of Freud's account of psychic life as a stalemated war between the superego and the id are only a little less oppressive.

The passions have found few champions among philosophers. Rousseau, who asserted that all natural inclination was good and that civilization was a kind of corruption, blotted his copybook somewhat by sending all his children to die in foundling homes in order that they would not disturb the busy work of his pen. Outside the academy, however, people have not looked so kindly on the notion that we would all be better off if the empire of reason were secure. Emotion has had no lack of support among literary men and is almost universally approved of by literary women, and the apologetic case they have presented has grown stronger over time. Rational men (not to mention rational supermen and Vulcans) are usually represented nowadays as moral defectives or unfortunate outsiders, unable to savor the delights of authentic human community. The tendency nowadays is to assert that the life of the undivided mind would hardly be worth living.

It is hardly surprising that preliterate cultures not much given to philosophising often had (and, where they have contrived to retain preliteracy, still have) myths which expressed this sense of fundamental division by linking men to animals. These myths are sometime just as complicated and as enigmatic as the work of the most esoteric philosophers, and the mysteries of totemism are difficult to unravel even for the cleverest anthropologists. There are, however, more straightforward representations which are easier to grasp—not merely for observers but, one must suppose, for their users. These include tales of shapeshifters who are periodically possessed and overwhelmed by animal spirits; myths of this kind are widespread, their usefulness presumably deriving from the fact that they are relatively easy to understand.

It is not surprising, either, that the activity of these animal spirits should be regarded with dire suspicion by people who find it possible to believe in them, even if they must deliberately suspend their disbelief in order to do so. Such suspicions are understandably at their direst when the animal spirits in question are identified with man's nearest rival for the top position in the food chain. In Europe, the second most dangerous predator in the woods was always the wolf, and it was the wolf which came to symbolize the most troublesome and the most dangerous animal spirits. It is for this reason that we—the literate descendants of superstitious ancestors—have converted a rich folklore of werewolves into a sturdy branch of horror fiction.

The literary history of werewolves is, in consequence, very long. It extends back at least as far as the *Satyricon* of Petronius, which was written mid-way through the first century A.D. There are werewolves in the romances

172

which were written to flatter the feudal barons of France—including those who were involved in the Norman conquest of Britain—and there are werewolves in the popular anecdotes that were recorded by overzealous witchfinders as evidence of the awful threat of devil-led heresy. There are werewolves in the Gothic fiction which sprang up so abundantly in the dark shadows cast by the Age of Enlightenment and there are werewolves in the "penny dreadfuls" which emerged in bold defiance of the price-fixing that was imposed on novels by Victorian circulating libraries struggling to keep their monopoly over the reading habit. Not until the twentieth century, however, did werewolves become common—and not until the twentieth century did they begin to undergo a metamorphosis of their own, from a simple figure of fear to something much more complicated and much more interesting.

* * * * * *

The literary depiction of werewolves is easy enough while they are the villains of the piece, appearing now as a subtly menacing human, now as an unsubtly vicious wolf. Such werewolves merely require their true nature to be made manifest, after which they can be consciencelessly shot. (The tradition which requires a silver bullet to do the job is of relatively recent provenance.) Any writer who wishes to make the werewolf into a protagonist, however, is faced with an awkward problem. Describing the werewolf's experience as a human being is straightforward, but describing his (or her) experience as a wolf is not.

The common opinion has always been that because wolves are not self-conscious, the wolfish experience could leave none but the merest memory-trace behind when the werewolf reverted to human form. Given that the common opinion also holds that transformation is an involuntary phenomenon brought on by the advent of the full moon, writers examining the werewolf from within can hardly help but see him (or her) as an unfortunate and unwitting victim of circumstance. As soon as writers began using werewolves as protagonists, therefore, they were bound to find a certain confusion creeping in to the image of evil incarnate.

In *The Wolf-Leader* (1857) Alexandre Dumas got around this difficulty by making his protagonist a willing party to a deal with the devil, which gives him the power to command and control a wolf-pack long before his slide into total corruption turns him into a werewolf. Robert Louis Stevenson's *Strange Case of Dr. Jekyll and Mr. Hyde* found a different solution, making the transformed Jekyll into a curious half-human being whose bestiality was not so complete as to exclude self-consciousness, which could therefore function as an adequate image of purified human evil. Rudyard Kipling's "The Mark of the Beast" (1891) is another tale which retains its moral fibre by refusing outright transformation; like many folkloristic tales, Kipling's represents the transformation as a literal curse, in this case vengeful rather than ancestral.

Throughout this early phase in the werewolf's literary history the wolfishness of the werewolf was primarily a matter of violence. The sexual component of passion—which had obtained marked expression in many folkloristic accounts of wolves and werewolves, including those associated with the many variants of "Little Red Riding Hood"—was inevitably de-emphasized by British writers laboring under the burden of Victorian taboos. Only the self-appointed radical G. W. M. Reynolds, in the penny dreadful *Wagner the Wehr-Wolf* (1846), incorporated an explicit sexual element into his villain's depredations, and even he was more concerned to link Wagner's exploits to the oppressive privileges of aristocracy.

The short-lived English Decadent movement of the 1890s began a change of emphasis, albeit in a subtle and calculatedly decorative fashion. Count Stanislaus Eric Stenbock's "The Other Side" (1893) is an encoded account of the onset of puberty confused by homoerotic impulses, while Clemence Housman's *The Were-Wolf* (1896) is a marvellous account of a doomed man's pursuit of female sexuality incarnate, as represented by the werewolf White Fell.

The abrupt beheading of the English Decadent Movement by the trial and imprisonment of Oscar Wilde resulted in a brief retreat into Edwardian coyness, but that could only be temporary. Extended literary studies of the werewolf often had them hunt in male/female pairs, like those in *The Door of the Unreal* (1919) by Gerald Biss and those in *Grey Shapes* (1937) by "Jack Mann" (E. Charles Vivian), in order that a sexual element might be unobtrusively added in.

By this time, of course, the cinematic wolf-man had made his debut. The principal reason for the divergent evolution of the literary werewolf and the movie wolf-man was, of course, the limitations imposed by the capability of special effects. To have a man change into an actual wolf was impractical, even if an adequately-trained alsatian or husky could be pressed into playing the part. Jekyll-and-Hyde type transformations were another matter, merely requiring a few time-lapse shots of gradually-enhanced make-up.

Adaptations of Stevenson's story were among Hollywood's most successful horror stories, from an artistic as well as a commercial point of view. It was not just that the actors playing the central part, from John Barrymore's silent version in 1920 through Fredric March in the 1931 version to Spencer Tracy in 1941, all put in spectacular performances, but that the scriptwriters' addition of a female victim added a cutting edge to the allegory which Stevenson had been forced by the tacit censorship of his day to omit. It was hardly surprising that the makers of *The Werewolf of London* (1935) should take pains to hire a "real actor" (Henry Hull) to play the part, nor that they should shape the story as a Stevensonesque melodrama of conscience and corruption.

The Wolf Man (1941) was a natural vehicle for Lon Chaney Jr., allowing him to reprise the make-up effects which had been his father's chief claim to fame. It was in this movie classic that the werewolf's status as a tormented victim was firmly and conclusively established as a stereotype, although literary works had been tending that way for some time. The pioneering exercise in lycanthropic existentialism, which not only allowed a werewolf to make a apologetic case for his plight but also to make substantial moral progress in turning his transformations to better ends was a series of tales by H. Warner Munn begun with "The Werewolf of Ponkert" (1925), which appeared at irregular intervals in the pulp magazine *Weird Tales* until 1931. *Weird Tales* also published more orthodox tales of werewolfish predation, but Munn's sympathies spread like a slow infection through the works of such writers as Seabury Quinn, whose later tales became rather more contemplative than his early account of nasty happenings at "The Phantom Farmhouse" (1923).

In *The Wolf Man*, as in all Hollywood films subject to the scrutiny of the Hays Office, the sexual subtext of the werewolf myth had to be handled with discretion even though it was the real heart of the story. The pantomime of screaming female chased and inarticulately abused by conscience-free wolf-man could be endlessly repeated but never analysed. The printed page provided much more scope. Guy Endore's account of *The Werewolf of Paris* (1933) begins with a little essay on the symbolic significance of the fact that brothels were called lupanars by the Romans and (occasionally) by the French, and goes on to provide a cunningly de-supernaturalized account of the career of a hapless werewolf, based on an actual account of the ghoulish exploits of one Sergeant Bertrand relocated to the brief but violent reign of the ill-fated Paris Commune of 1870-71.

Endore's Bertrand is briefly enabled to control his lusts with the aid of a patient whore, but even when it escapes those bounds his desperate intercourse with freshly-buried corpses is a blissfully innocent pastime by comparison with the everyday atrocities committed by his sane comrades-in-arms. It is with this neatly devastating argument that the real redemption of the werewolf from the curse of excessive morality began.

Two of the most remarkable werewolf stories to appear in the American pulps were written by Jack Williamson. The first of them, "Wolves of Darkness" (1932), is the most phantasmagoric of all pulp horror stories featuring werewolves, showing the influence of A. Merritt's lush escapist fantasies as well as employing pseudoscientific notions borrowed from the fledgling SF genre to provide an apologetic jargon. To what extent it drew upon the author's own nightmares it is impossible to say, but Williamson has taken to trouble to place on record the fact that the subject-matter and development of his subsequent werewolf novel *Darker Than You Think* (1940) was considerably affected by the psycho-analysis that he underwent in the meantime.

In *Darker Than You Think* the hero who is initially intimidated by the sexy female werewolf is eventually con-verted to her cause when he is brought to realise that he and she are of the same species, set aside from the common herd of humanity—whose members no longer have the power to make fruitful connection with their animal spirits. Here the hero is an explicit victim of repression, whose first task is to liberate his submerged potential, and only then to win full conscious control over its expression. This was to establish a highly significant benchmark for future accounts of the di-vided self which elected to use the werewolf motif.

* * * * * * *

Modern werewolf stories have followed this trend through to its various logical conclusions. The link between lycanthropy and the upsurge of "animal spirits" associated with puberty was made symbolically explicit in the best of all werewolf films, *The Company of Wolves* (1984), devel-oped from two short stories by Angela Carter. This was fol-lowed a year later by *Teenwolf* (1985), which turned the ab-surd melodrama of *I Was a Teenage Werewolf* (1957) into equally absurd comedy.

By this time, of course, cinematic special effects had become more than equal to the task of producing extreme transformations, the impressive metamorphoses of *An American Werewolf in London* (1979) providing a precedent that was prolifically echoed in *The Howling* (1981), albeit in a slightly compromised fashion which allowed its monsters to walk erect.

The Howling made much of its psychoanalytic so-phistication, imagining a whole community of werewolves keeping more-or-less careful control of their proclivities un-til their cover is blown when one of their number becomes a serial sex-killer, but its final scene—in which the infected female newsreader turns into a ridiculously cute wolfette on

177

screen and begs to be put out of her misery—represents a craven submission to backward-harking forces of demonization. The much inferior "sequels" which followed in 1985 and 1987 progressively converted the horror element back to comedy; the Australia-made *The Howling III* struck an intriguingly novel note of absurdity in making its female werewolf a marsupial who carries her baby around in a pouch.

Once this injection of psychoanalytic "insight" had been absorbed by the cinematic mainstream it was only a matter of time before *Wolf* (1994) emerged—with Jack Nicholson playing the lead in his inimitably mannered style—to produce a slyly ironic tale in which a dose of lycanthropy provides a welcome and necessary boost to the kind of nice guy who is in danger of losing out in the dog-eat-dog world of modern business, while sending the kind of bad guy who thrives in such a context over the edge into barking madness.

In fiction, meanwhile, many werewolves were fighting a much better-organized and better-balanced fight against stigmatization, and painstakingly attempting—not altogether successfully—to channel their more violent urges into enterprises that were at least arguably legitimate. Notable examples of this kind of enterprise include *The Nightwalker* (1979) by Thomas Tessier, *The Wolf's Hour* (1989) by Robert McCammon, and *Moon Dance* (1989) by S. P. Somtow. Angela Carter's stories in which young females learn to accept the implicit wolfishness of sexuality were echoed in other feminist parables, including Tanith Lee's *Lycanthia; or, The Children of Wolves* (1981)—one of several stories capitalising on ethological studies which had revealed that wolf packs are actually led and organized by their dominant females—and Suzy McKee Charnas's gleefully graphic "Boobs" (1989), which "explains" the monthly cycle of lycanthropic metamorphosis in a manner that must always have been obvious although it had long been allowed to lie scrupulously unmentioned.

This rehabilitation of the werewolf has run parallel to the rehabilitation of the vampire as described in the previous chapter, but the werewolf has not extended its influence into lifestyle fantasy in the way that vampire imagery has. This is testimony to the fact that the werewolf remains a more problematic symbol, more intimately bound to our rapt contemplation of our own inner nature. Ironically, the clearest demonstration of this oppressive intimacy is to be found in one of the most eccentric manifestations of the imagery—a monumental exercise in self-indulgence whose like will probably never be seen again. The item in question is Michael Jackson's *Thriller* video (1984).

The opening sequence of the *Thriller* video is a pastiche of a 1950s horror film in which a hesitant boy who has driven a shy girl to a remote spot explains that he is "not like other guys." She naturally takes this to mean that he is no mere sexual predator, and that his intentions are essentially honorable, but the audience knows better. As the face of the moon is revealed and the boy turns into a Chaneyesque wolfman the point of view pulls back and shows us a cinema audience watching the scene. Here, a boy likewise played by Michael Jackson (but now dressed in contemporary fashion) is wolfing popcorn and thoroughly enjoying himself; his girlfriend, by contrast, is disturbed by what she sees and is not reassured by his mocking observation that "it's just a film." She insists on leaving the cinema, and he promises to see her safely home.

It is while this boy and girl walk through the dark streets that Jackson begins to sing. The conventions of musical cinema allow the scene to shift instantly from a naturalistic mode to a highly artificial one. The lyric of the song initially echoes the protective role that the boy has tacitly assumed but soon begins to shift into a different mood. It is interrupted by a phantasmagoric sequence introduced by Vincent Price reading a brief poem in his typical mock-horrific style, in which rotting corpses emerge from graves and the boy and girl are gradually surrounded by a whole troupe of cinematic monsters more reminiscent of the visceral tradition introduced by *Night of the Living Dead* (1968) than the weak-kneed images of the 1950s. When the girl turns to the boy for the promised protection, however, he is already becoming one of them.

The transformed Jackson leads a chorus of dancing ghouls while singing the remainder of the song, whose assertive lyric now boasts that he can give the girl a much bigger thrill than any mere horror film. The central assumption embedded in his claim is, of course, that the excitement derived from horror fiction is a covert kind of sexual arousal which cannot measure up to the "real thing." The girl, intimidated by the messengers if not by the message, flees in terror— only to find that there is no safe haven, and that neither doors nor floorboards can hold the monsters at bay. As her situation becomes desperate, the narrative point of view shifts again.

This time, the horrific vision becomes a dream from which she is awakening, to find the boy once again assuming a protectively reassuring role. Yet again he tells her that everything will be fine—but it is no surprise to the audience that when he turns away to favor the camera with a knowing look he does so with the glowing eyes of some predatory monster. The paradoxical point of this final move is to persuade us— and no one knew, at the time, just how desperate Michael Jackson was to become in trying to make the point—that he really is, after all, exactly like other guys, in that whatever one might say about about true love and authentic respect, the wolf within will still expect to be fed.

* * * * * * *

The werewolf of phase one of the *Thriller* video, like Lon Chaney Jr.'s wolf-man or Michael Landon's teenage werewolf, is a young male who looks with stern disapproval, if not with naked terror, upon the tendencies of his own sexuality. He wishes, desperately, that he were different. The amber-eyed predator of phase three, on the other hand, is slyly but utterly unrepentant. He knows what he is and has accepted it. As Robert Bly was later to recommend in *Iron John*, he has made peace with "the hairy man within"; he has shed the uncomfortable burden of moral responsibility. Unlike the heroines of *The Company of Wolves* and *Wolf*, however his female counterpart has not. Perhaps she should,

180

and perhaps she will, but the question remains awkwardly in the balance.

Just as the exploits of contemporary vampires serve to remind us that the most intimate and loving human relationships retain an element of parasitic exploitation, so the exploits of contemporary werewolves serve to remind us that those same relationships retain an element of greedy predation. The persistence of the werewolf as a literary and cinematic image, and its dogged refusal to shake off its horrific connotations, further undermines the pernicious myth—which remains central to romantic fiction—that love is a kind of saving grace, builds protective walls around a relationship that time cannot erode nor emotional upheavals shatter. The ever-presence of the werewolf reminds us that it is never sufficient to keep the wolf from the door, because its kindred spirit already dwells within, ready to respond to every ominous brightening of the night.

Even if we are to conclude that Plato was wrong in calling for the annihilation of the "lower appetites"—on the grounds that a precious baby would be thrown out with the dirty bathwater—we have to admit that Rousseau was wrong too. Nature is not intrinsically good, nor savagery intrinsically noble. The animal spirits which drive and distract us do indeed have a wolfish component, which requires appeasement as well as secure housing.

It is not clear, even in these psychoanalytically enlightened times, what the best solution to a werewolf's existential plight might be, but if the record of thought-experiment provided by fiction has produced any clear conclusions at all, one of them is surely that begging to be blown away by a silver bullet is no solution at all. We really do have to live with our inner wolves.

NOTES

CHAPTER III

[1]A more detailed analysis of the term "scientific romance" and its application can be found in Brian Stableford, *Scientific Romance in Britain, 1890-1950*. London: Fourth Estate, 1985.

[2]"Murray Constantine" was a pen name used by Katherine Burdekin, who also published some scientific romances under her own name.

CHAPTER V

[1] Buranelli, Vincent. *Edgar Allan Poe*. New York: Twayne, 1977, p. 46-47. *Eureka: A Prose Poem* was published in New York by Putnam in 1848; the first French translation by Charles Baudelaire was issued in Paris by Levy in 1864.

[2]See, for instance, Sheffield's *Between the Strokes of Night*. New York: Baen, 1985, p. 344-46.

[3]See, for instance, van Vogt's *Voyage of the Space Beagle*. New York: Simon & Schuster, 1950.

[4]Wilson, William. *A Little Earnest Book Upon a Great Old Subject*. London: Darton & Co., 1851, p. 132-35.

[5]Serviss, Garrett P. *Curiosities of the Sky*. New York: Harper & Brothers, 1909, p. xv.

[6]Flammarion, Camille. *Lumen*. London: William Heinemann, 1897, p. 168-69. This essay-cum-story first appeared in *Récits de l'infini: Lumen, histoire d'une âme; Histoire d'une comète; Dans l'infini*, published in Paris by Didier in 1873, but may have been written as early as

1865. References to later editions of the collection, including those published by E. Flammarion after 1885, give the third item as "La Vie universelle et éternelle," but I have been unable to ascertain whether this is actually a different story or a retitling of "Dans l'infini." The first English translation was *Stories of Infinity*, translated by S. R. Crocker. Boston: Roberts, 1873. The expanded version of *Lumen* was published separately in France by E. Flammarion in 1887; the translation into English by A. A. M. & R. M. was published by Heinemann in 1897, and is said by the publisher to have some new material.

CHAPTER VI

[1]Squire, J. C. "Introduction" to *If It Had Happened Otherwise*. London: Longmans, 1932, p. viii.

CHAPTER VIII

[1]Chesney, George C. "The Battle of Dorking," in *The Battle of Dorking Controversy*. London: Cornmarket Reprints, 1972, p. 60-61.

[2]Tracy, Louis. *The Final War*. London: C. Arthur Pearson, 1896, p. 348.

[3]Childers, M. A. "Note" added to the fourteenth impression of *The Riddle of the Sands*, by Erskine Childers. London: Sidgwick & Jackson, 1931, p. v.

[4]Churchill, Winston. Speech made at Dundee in 1922, quoted in *Bestseller* by Claud Cockburn. London: Sidgwick & Jackson, 1972, p. 78.

CHAPTER XI

[1]Frayling, Christopher. *Vampires: Lord Byron to Count Dracula*. London: Faber & Faber, 1991, p. 95.

INDEX

Brave New World (Huxley), 47, 126-127
"The Bride of Korinth" (Goethe), 138
"The Bride of the Grave" (anon.), 159
"A Brief History of Vampires" (Stableford), 7-8, 159-169
"A Brief History of Werewolves" (Stableford), 7-8, 171-181
Bring the Jubilee (Moore), 77
Brite, Poppy Z., 165, 167
"The British and American Traditions of Speculative Fiction" (Stableford), 6, 41-52
British Interplanetary Society, 124-125
British Science Fiction Association, 95
British SF magazines, 93-103
Brown, Douglas, 77
Browning, Tod, 161, 163
Brunner, John, 62, 79, 81, 101
Bruno, Giordano, 73
Buchan, John, 111
Budspy (Dvorkin), 78
Bug Jack Barron (Spinrad), 102
Bulmer, Kenneth "Ken," 99-100
Buranelli, Vincent, 67-68
Burgoyne, Alan H., 76
The Burning Mountain (Coppel), 78
Burroughs, Edgar Rice, 43, 122, 143, 145
Burton, Robert, 131, 151
Die Büsche der Pandora—SEE: *Pandora's Box*
Byrne, Eugene, 82-83
Byron, George Gordon, Lord, 150-151, 161, 169
Cabell, James Branch, 144
Callenbach, Ernest, 61
Calmet, Dom Augustine, 150-157, 160
Campbell, H. J. "Bert," 100
Campbell, John W., Jr., 49, 125
Capek, Karel, 126
The Captain of the 'Mary Rose' (Clowes), 109
Card, Orson Scott, 83, 89
"Carmilla" (Le Fanu), 141, 161-162
Carnell, Ted, 94, 97-98, 101
Carter, Angela, 146, 177-178
A Case of Conscience (Blish), 58
Cazotte, Jacques, 138
"The Celestial Plot" (Borges and Bioy Casares), 85
"Centre for the Study of Metaphor," 6
Chadwick, Philip George, 115
Chalker, Jack, 79-80
Chamberlin, Joseph, 75
Chambers, Robert W., 143
Chaney, Lon, Jr., 175-176, 179-180

188

190

Disney, Walt, 27
d'Israeli, Isaac, 75
Dissertations sur les apparitions des anges, des démons et des esprits—
   SEE: *The Phantom World*
"The Diversifal" (Rocklynne), 79
The Divide (Overgard), 78
"Dolores" (Swinburne), 142
The Door of the Unreal (Biss), 175
Doppelgangers (Heard), 47
Downtiming the Night Side (Chalker), 79-80
Downward to Earth (Silverberg), 59
Doyle, Arthur Conan, 77, 88, 95, 141
Dr. Jekyl and Mr. Hyde—SEE: *Strange Case of Dr. Jekyl and Mr. Hyde*
Dracula (Stoker), 88, 160-165, 168
Dracula (film), 161, 163
The Dracula Tape (Saberhagen), 165
"Dracula's Guest" (Stoker), 162
The Dragon—SEE: *The Yellow Peril*
Dragul—SEE: Vlad Tepes
"Draka" series (Stirling), 81
"The Dream Theatre" (musical group), 167
Druid's Blood (Friesner), 88
Dublin University Magazine, 161
Dumas, Alexandre, 174
Dune series (Herbert), 62
Dvorkin, David, 78
Dwellers in the Mirage (Merritt), 144
The Earth Again Redeemed (Green), 84
Earth-Spirit (Wedekind), 140
Ecotopia (Callenbach), 61
Eight Keys to Eden (Clifton), 61
Einstein, Albert, 73, 122-123
Eklund, Gordon, 83
Elizium (musical album), 167
Elleander Morning (Yulsman), 78
Ellison, Harlan, 9
Elsie Venner (Holmes), 143
Emperor of the If (Dent), 85
The Empire of Fear (Stableford), 85
"The Empress of the Earth"—SEE: *The Yellow Danger*
Encyclopedia of Science Fiction (ed. Nicholls and Clute), 7, 90-91
The End of Eternity (Asimov), 79
The End of the World (Flammarion), 54-55
Endore, Guy, 176
An Englishman's Castle (television), 78
Enlightenment, 155
"Ensemble of Shadows" (musical group), 167
An Epic of Women (O'Shaughnessy), 142

French literature, 139-141, 162-163
Freud, Sigmund, 31, 145-146, 162-163, 171
Friesner, Esther, 88
From the Earth to the Moon (Verne), 118
Froude, James Anthony, 70
The Future Eve (Villiers de L'Isle-Adam), 139-140
future war stories, 42-45, 77-78, 105-116, 118-119
Futuristic Stories, 97, 99
futurology, 117-128
Galaxy, 98
Gamow, George, 85-86
Garden of Eden, 61
Garrett, Randall, 89
The Gas War of 1940 (Bell), 43, 115—SEE ALSO: *Valiant Clay*
Gaskell, Jane, 164, 166
The Gate of Worlds (Silverberg), 81
Gautier, Théophile, 139, 159-160, 162
Geoffrey, Louis-Napoléon, 76-77
Gerald G. Swan Publishers, 96
Gernsback, Hugo, 41, 44-45, 95, 125
Gibson, William, 88
Gillings, Walter, 95, 97-98
Gingrich, Newt, 91
"The Girl in the Golden Atom" (Cummings), 143
The Girl in the Moon (film), 124
"The Girl with the Hungry Eyes" (Leiber), 145
Gladstone, William Ewart, 106
"The Glass of Blood" (Lorrain), 163
Glenarvon (Lamb), 161
Gloag, John, 43, 45-47, 115
Goethe, Johann Wolfgang von, 138
"The Gold Bug" (Poe), 71, 73
"The Golden Flower-Pot" (Hoffmann), 138
"Der Goldene Topf"—SEE: "The Golden Flower-Pot"
Golding, William, 22
Gothic punk sub-culture, 166-167
The Gothic Society, 167
Gourmont, Rémy de, 140, 153, 163
Goyne, Richard, 97
Graeme, Bruce, 77
Grandier, Urbain, 140, 154
"The Great God Pan" (Machen), 141
The Great War—SEE: World War I
The Great War in England in 1897 (Le Queux), 109-110
The Great War of 189- (Colomb, *et al.*), 108
"The Great War of 1892" (Colomb, *et al.*), 108
"Great Work of Time" (Crowley), 80
"Greater Than Gods" (Moore), 79

194

206

9780809519118